THE SELF-HEALING SPIRAL

HEAL AND LOVE YOURSELF

ELEONORE DE POSSON

THE SELF-HEALING SPIRAL

HEAL AND LOVE YOURSELF

INTRODUCTION

One afternoon in June 2018, I completely broke down.

It's Friday, I'm exhausted. I can't keep on smiling and pretending I'm fine. I go home to escape everything. I lay down on my bed and close my eyes for a few minutes, but when I open them, I feel even worse.

I feel lonely. I'm losing it. It's like everything is collapsing around me. Nothing happens as planned. Nothing is going in the right direction. Life is happening in front of me, but I'm not in control of it. I can't do this anymore. I don't have the strength to fight anymore. I feel empty, weak, out of breath. The thoughts keep cascading through my mind.

I'm starting to feel dizzy and try to sit up on the bed. Something is happening. My heart beats faster and faster. My breath is short, I struggle to breathe. My feet and hands tingle. I feel like I'm going to die. I want to die. Life has no purpose. What is the point of all this? It's too much. I won't be able to rebuild everything. I'm losing it.

I'm having my first panic attack.

Four months earlier, my husband left me after 6 months of marriage. I did not see it coming. I thought we were happy and full of dreams for the future. When I returned from a Yoga Teacher Training in India, he told me he was happier without me. He had realized that he did not love me and had, in fact, never loved me. He loved someone else.

The emotional violence of the next few days consumed me slowly. I didn't understand. I couldn't accept. I could not give up this man who I had given my life to. The more I resisted, the more his harsh words destroyed me. My life was collapsing just when I thought I had reached a peak of love, joy, and inner peace.

The panic attack had happened to tell me that the "work" was not finished. I went back to my day job, gave yoga classes, and went out every night to rebuild a social life. Keeping myself busy, I was feeling alive again. I had put the dark thoughts, sadness and suffering aside. I did not think about it anymore, or rather, I did not want to think about it any more. I just wanted to be strong and happy. I wanted to regain the joyful peak I had lost on February 28th.

A few days after the panic attack of that Friday afternoon, I realized that I was experiencing a relapse. I could no longer fill myself with activities to avoid feeling the pain and pretend everything was fine. I had become the loser of my own game. It was then that I accepted that my healing could not be done in the blink of an eye. It would be longer than I had hoped. I could not recover from such a trauma in four months, even if I felt like it. Finally, I dared to look inside. I dared to see what I had been repressing for several months. I allowed my emotions to *be*.

The beginning of a magnificent introspection took place. I truly wanted to understand everything I was going through. I went to therapy with a psychologist, engrossed myself in books, practised yoga and meditation daily. I spent a lot of time asking myself all the questions of the world. My observations turned inward rather than outward. My only goal was to understand and decipher the emotions that inhabited me. I finally dared to go through this stage, embracing my pain and approaching my suffering with compassion.

I was afraid of my own fears sometimes. I did not know how to handle the emotions that overwhelmed me. They seemed insurmountable and I did not think I had the strength to live with them. Abandonment, rejection, betrayal, humiliation, sadness, misunderstanding, anger, frustration, shame, fear of loving again, fear of my own feelings, fear of myself... There was a lot to talk about, digest and accept. But, how to get better? How to heal? How to trust myself again? How to find my way? How to dare to love again? How could I possibly take the risk of having my heart broken again? I was alone in this desire to understand without having any idea where to start.

Over the weeks, I learned to tame my emotions. I felt better, even though the panic attacks returned regularly. The box had been opened. I wanted something that, in just a few minutes, would allow me to turn those uncomfortable emotions into a more comfortable, manageable state. I tried several things before I understood how I worked. All these tools helped me progress. The support of my loved ones was infallible and I thank them again today with these words. But, that wasn't it yet.

Life continued to challenge me by offering me to move to Canada. I threw myself into this opportunity with a feeling of absolute freedom. I had no idea that I was going to have another difficult time with myself. Such uprooting wasn't easy. I continued my search for this tool, this set of tools, this process that would allow me to always do the right thing for me.

One October morning, as I woke up, I had a eureka moment. That was it! Everything I had learned and discovered lately was coming together. All the dots suddenly connected. I had just found the thing that allowed me to systematically transform these unpleasant emotions. Was it really that? I wrote, gathered the ideas, and verified the elements against proven theories.

At the next anxious moment, I tested it. It worked! It really worked!

I named this method the Self-Healing Spiral. In this book of the same title, I share the method that allowed me to heal week after week. This method is made of six steps. Three stages are inactive. These are stages that we are simply going through and bring more self-awareness. The three others offer practical tools, that are accessible to all, easy and beneficial. Together, they form the Self-Healing Circle. By going through this circle several times, day after day, you heal and rise up the Self-Healing Spiral.

Although the Self-Healing Spiral comes from my own experience, it is based on many theories that have been scientifically proven. I gathered them methodically to create this strategy for myself first. It offered me the peace I was looking for and that's why I share it today. I sincerely believe that the Self-Healing Spiral is a simple but powerful concept for anyone who wants to be more comfortable with their emotions, overcome certain blockages and learn to love themselves. This book will open new doors and bring you both theoretical knowledge and practical tools to progress on your healing path. It will restore your power, your joy, your love and your trust in yourself and in life.

Finally, I suggest you read the following pages with lightness and pleasure. Taking care of yourself should be fun and comforting. Amongst all the tools that will be presented, you can choose those which seem the most appropriate for you. You may want to try them all. Some you might not like, others you will love. There is no good or bad. Use this book as you wish. If you want to do things differently, adapt the exercises to your liking, do not hesitate to do so. Follow your intuition because it always takes you to the right place. All I need is your willingness to try, to discover yourself and to learn new things.

I hope that you will devour these pages, be patient and trust the Self-Healing Spiral, which will make you realize that you already have everything in you.

1

PRESENTATION OF THE SELF-HEALING SPIRAL

L ife is made of ups and downs, pains and pleasures, happy and sad experiences. It is a reflection of our conscious and unconscious inner world. It is made up of opportunities to open our eyes to who we really are so that we can learn to deeply love ourselves. The path of life is strewn with unpleasant experiences to awaken our desire to know ourselves, heal and truly flourish. For me, it was a divorce. For others, it might be an accident, an illness or another challenging event. These episodes open the door to ourselves. We are hurt and are looking for answers. The need for understanding and strong emotions finally force introspection. Our healing pushes us to make different choices. We then create a life that is more aligned with who we really are. We can be a lot of things and have a lot of different lives. The possibilities are endless. These uncomfortable experiences, if understood properly, will bring us closer to the life that allows our soul to flourish.

However, I don't think it is necessary to go through this

journey with so much suffering. It is possible to accept that each setback is, in fact, an opportunity to discover and love ourselves. We are then ready to dance with life. Life is our partner. The choreography is made of our thoughts, choices and actions. I believe that the best way to dance with life is to fully live in symphony with your emotions and understand them. Living with our emotions is key to help us understand and love ourselves. Let's dare to meet the emotions that come our way.

The Self-Healing Spiral teaches this. It shows us how to welcome our emotions; to overcome blockages and improve our relationship with ourselves; finally, and most importantly, to heal our physical, emotional, mental and spiritual wounds. In this chapter you will discover the six consecutive steps of the Self-Healing Circle. You will be shown why they follow each other and what each step brings to the whole. You will also understand how the series of Self-Healing Circles unite to create, together, a Spiral that leads to self-love and healing.

The Self-Healing Circle

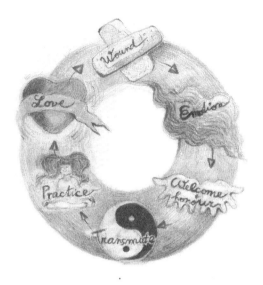

The Self-Healing Spiral consists of two elements: The Self-Healing Circle and The Self-Healing Spiral. A spiral is composed of several circles that never close but follow each other to rise or fall. Healing is not fast. It is not linear either. On the contrary, it is cyclical. We think we have moved on and then face it again a few weeks later. We feel stuck at the same place, move a little forward, then move backwards. In fact, we are exactly at the right place: our wounds contain many layers. They are like an onion. Before getting to the heart of a wound and healing it deeply, we need patience and compassion to peel away the layers. We will welcome the same emotions over and over again, every time at a different layer of the wound. The more we go round the circle, the more our wounds fade. The more they fade, the more we rise up the Self-Healing Spiral. The more we rise, the better we feel.

The Self-Healing Circle is composed of 6 stages. An event arises and leads us to the first stage: The Wound. The sixth and last stage of the Circle is that of Love. It's the greatest one because it is what allows the movement of the Spiral. Indeed, this love will join the first stage of the wound and heal it, because o*nly love heals*. The more we love ourselves, the more we heal, the more we rise up the Self-Healing Spiral. We're talking about self-love here. The love of others undoubtedly helps us to gain self-confidence and there is nothing like feeling deeply loved, but we are the only ones capable of giving ourselves all the love we need. This love is healing and we will see that in details further on. Let's do a little exercise together to get to the heart of the matter. Take a pen, a piece of paper, a notebook or even answer below with a figure from I to IO:

- How much do you trust yourself?
- How much do you accept yourself?
- How much do you love yourself?

Put this book down and take some time to *really* think about it. Do it to start your own healing process. Reading is great, but putting what you read into action will make the difference. I guess by now you're holding a pen. Be honest with yourself and write the answers down. Keep them in a safe place as we will come back to them at the end of your reading.

The works of Masaru Emoto[1] and Dr. Laskow[2] have largely proven that the Energy of Love is a source of healing. Both of them have meticulously analyzed the reactions of natural elements, such as water, when they were subjected to vibrations of love. By vibration of love, I mean the expression of feelings by saying words such as "thank you" or "I love you". The results are inspiring as they found out that the elements receiving love vibrations created more beautiful shapes, grew or healed faster. This was not the case for elements receiving words of hatred or ignorance.

In addition, Love is the only source of deep healing because our wounds have taken root in an experience, involving the separation of two human beings, felt as a lack of love. Whether it is in fact a lack of love or the perception of it, the consequences are the same because the brain does not distinguish reality from thought (see chapter 5). These hurtful experiences begin in our early childhood. While we are barely a few months old, we need love and affection to survive. If we do not feel this love at a given moment, it leaves a trace and creates a wound. For example, we are ignored so we might feel rejected. This childhood wound is slowly crafting our personality and so we will easily feel rejected by others. Whether it's a breakup, a divorce, a job turning out badly, an argument or a personal failure, these milestones are meant to make us grow up and gain awareness of this wound that needs healing.

The wounds are expressed through emotions; this is stage two of the Self-Healing Circle. We feel fear, sadness, despair, melancholy, disappointment... All these uncomfortable emotions appear for the simple reason that they are the visible part of the iceberg called Wound. They tell us that we must look after ourselves. They rise to the surface to free us from a weight and put us on the healing path. They play the role of the Healer. Every emotion has its own mission and its own message. Once we understand their importance, we dare to give them their rightful place. We allow ourselves to welcome and honour them as they deserve.

Embracing our emotions is the only way to progress on the healing path. There's no shortcut, although I thought I had found many. In Western society we're taught to hold back our tears and cries of anger. We must always look good and keep emotions to ourselves: "keep calm and carry on." So, how are we supposed to welcome and honour what happens inside of us? That's what we address in step three, "Welcome and Honour". We will see how to take care of the emotion at the level of our heart. We'll discover different tools to address the rising anger, the sadness that invades us and the disappointment that pierces us. We'll learn to feel safe with our emotions and observe that when they are welcomed properly, they will go away just minutes later.

Step four is the tipping point of the Self-Healing Circle. The first three stages of the Circle bring unpleasant emotions to life. The next three express pleasant emotions. Indeed, the "Transmute" stage symbolizes the transition from shadow to light. It projects us into a joyful future, rewires our beliefs and deconstructs our fears. This step takes care of the emotion at the level of the mind. This is where we take our power back and realize that we are the artists of our own lives.

Once heaviness is replaced by lightness, we arrive at step 5: the "Practice". The emotion felt previously has settled in our body and tightened our muscles. It is necessary to discharge this physical tension from ourselves. Step five takes care of the emotion at the level of the body. It offers different tools to let the emotion circulate and clean ourselves energetically from it. Moreover, this practice will move us towards more love and joy of being ourselves.

Finally, we reach the last stage of the Self-Healing Circle: "Love". In order to heal our wound and let it close for good, we must increase the love we have for ourselves. This love will have grown thanks to the attention we gave ourselves during stages 3, 4 and 5. To love yourself is to take care of yourself in all circumstances. To love yourself is to accept yourself totally and deeply, exactly as you are. This is the purpose of life. *Live to love yourself, love yourself to live.*

As you have just discovered, The Self-Healing Circle is made of 6 stages. Three of the stages occur naturally and are inactive but bring about awareness. These are steps one, two and six, the Wound, Emotion and Love, respectively. The other three stages are active, meaning they require action: this is where you come in and make a difference. Steps three, four, and five: Welcome and Honour, Transmute, and Practice. They offer a variety of tools that you can choose from to best heal your wounds. These will directly impact the three inactive steps. The Self-Healing Circle makes us realize that we have our well-being in our hands.

This is where the circle ends. By applying the principles and tools provided, you will know how to take care of yourself. How to manage your emotions, to welcome what is happening inside of you, to overcome certain blockages and to improve your relationship with yourself. In this state of well-being, you will make better decisions for your life and inevitably increase the love for yourself. This will heal your wounds and help you live a more fulfilling life. You may have noticed that the steps create more than a circle, they create a virtuous circle, which continues to rise. It is a Self-Healing Spiral.

The Self-Healing Spiral

The Self-Healing Spiral presents healing as an elevation. It brings us closer to our very essence, raising our consciousness. We are no longer in reaction, but act by listening to our inner voice and know what's right for us. It consists of several circles that flow into each other, as you can see in the drawing. We can easily go up or down the Spiral according to how we face life's challenges.

The higher we are in the Spiral, the more fulfilled we are. The lower we are in the Spiral, the more exposed the wounds are. At any time, we can go down again in the Self-

Healing Spiral. Life will make us navigate between these circles. The goal is not to stay at the top. It would be misleading to think that one can stay there, avoiding suffering. The goal is to learn to go back up when we find ourselves in a dark place with heavy emotions. This dark place is where I was before creating the Self-Healing Spiral. We all experience, at least once in our lives, this dark, double-locked house. We isolate ourselves, but the light always ends up piercing through the shutters.

The Self-Healing Spiral acts like the law of attraction. This universal law demonstrates that our outer world is a reflection of our inner world. We reap what we sow. Our thoughts, intentions and actions create our life. Their vibrations create constantly. The more we come to love and accept ourselves as we are, the more beautiful things happen to us. This law may seem abstract to you at this stage, but it will open the doors of the energetic world. This invisible world impacts us much more than one might think. We all tend to believe only what we see. Unfortunately, this limits us because the human eye only sees 2% of everything that's happening around it. Rather than believing what you see, I suggest you reverse the exercise and see what you believe. So, what do you see now?

What we learned from this chapter:

- The Self-Healing Spiral consists of flowing circles, each composed of 6 steps.
- The Self-Healing Spiral is a method that helps us manage our emotions, take care of ourselves, overcome blockages, love and heal ourselves.
- Only love heals. Different tools in this book will

show us the way and guide us to the top of the Spiral.

- Our life is a reflection of our inner world, where we attract what we consciously and unconsciously believe, in order to discover ourselves. We then learn to love ourselves deeply as we are.

2

STEP 1: THE WOUND

L et me tell you one of my favourite bedtime stories:

A gigantic cloud made of love and kindness wants to spread more love around him. He creates, other than himself, many little clouds to which he wants to teach plenty of things. He gives each little cloud the choice of their studies. From a long list, they choose if they wish to learn to trust, set boundaries, no longer be saviours, overcome feelings of rejection, and so on. They have options for everything, but they must also register for the main class: Learning to Love Oneself.

Once the little clouds chose their studies, they meet at the Grand Book Shop of Gifts to fill up their backpacks with as many resources as possible to succeed in their studies. They receive wisdom, empathy, creativity, ingenuity,... Each one receives the resources needed to succeed in their studies and the main class.

Once ready, the little clouds get on the bus taking them to the School of Life. Rather quickly, conversations begin and friend-ships are formed. Some even promise to find each other between classes to exchange notes and help to succeed in their studies. The bus starts making its way, moving at full speed. The journey lulls the little clouds to sleep. On waking, they have completely forgotten which studies they wanted to pursue and what was in their backpacks.

But, fortunately, the answers hide deep inside them. The adventure promises to be beautiful and eventful!

Dolorès Lamarre[1] recounted this little story to me. It marvellously illustrates my vision of Life. It elates my child-like heart as well as the little cloud inside me. Although it appears simplistic, it is strong in this simplicity.

We have all come into the world with wounds and gifts. It is fascinating to observe new-borns and to note that some are calm, others independent, some cry a lot, others love to sleep. Though we may only be a few days old, our tempera-ment is already visible. We are all unique and different. You might say that it's because of our parents' DNA. We have the same character traits and confirm them from our first few days. In reality, I believe it goes much further: we have chosen our parents for their character traits and their unhealed wounds. We carry the same wounds as our parents and that's not because we inherited them. It is because we also have things to bring them on this journey. Our healing will allow them to heal as well.

Why am I in this body and in my family? Why is *this* person in *this* body in *this* family? The question will remain eternally debatable and there are probably as many answers as there are people on Earth. I share my own answer with you to stimulate reflection. But, in the end, there may not be a correct answer. We are in this body and one of this family. Trying to understand why will not change that situation. We can only be aware of it and from there, discover the unknown that we are and learn to love ourselves.

Our gifts help us on this rocky path. Our gifts are char-acter traits and unique competences that we develop throughout our life. They are ours and have been entrusted to us so that we can, at our turn, offer them to the world. Our gifts are here to be gifted. They bring something unique to those who can receive them. They put us at joy just for being ourselves. When we fully flourish in what we like to do, then we share these gifts. Thus, we are elated to get up each morning: life fills itself with colours; we love ourselves exactly as we are. Serving the world with our gifts is what will fulfil us and heal our wounds. This is the reason we have reunited here: the healing of our wounds and the joy of being ourselves through the sharing of our gifts.

. . .

Life always stays in perfect balance

Life is a magnificent equation that always stays in perfect balance. You can be sure of it by just looking at the perfection of nature. The seasons, the ecosystem, the food chain – their beauty and perfect functioning fascinate me. Science, and its numerous studies, brings answers to our needs of understanding the world and places this perfect balance in the spotlight. The only unknown factor in this grand equation is us.

This goes even deeper. On a human level, this grand equation is made up of 7.5 billion little equations. We each have our own one, composed of our own vision of the world, our way of reacting to experiences, our personality, qualities and faults. We all live in our own world and each world has its own equation that depends on the unknown.

The equation depends on the unknown and the unknown finds itself through the perfect balance of the equation. To form itself, the other elements implement themselves in order to present us with clues – events – that will teach us things about this beautiful unknown. You might be asking yourself why we need to try and discover the unknown. If we turn back to the bedtime story, it is in order to pass these studies and particularly the main class: learning to love oneself. Because when we love ourselves, we share these gifts and become part of the perfection of life. We are one. We enter in the unity of love and this is where deep healing takes place.

So, this unknown, equipped with its backpack filled with qualities and flaws, gifts and wounds, will attract the necessary motions to discover oneself. If the equation doesn't get moving, the unknown cannot be discovered. If it moves, if we live, interact with others, walk, fall, love, suffer, surrender, trust and get back up, we discover little by little the contents of the unknown.

Wounds and their Masks

The open wounds we have are like a pair of glasses: we see life through their lenses. We interpret events completely differently depending on what glasses we wear. These differences open our eyes towards our wounds. In fact, a break-up could be experienced as either an injustice or a rejection depending on our personal equation. Lise Bourbeau, a Quebecois author, wrote a fascinating thesis on this subject.[2] After years of consultations, she found that five different types of wounds exist: rejection, abandonment, humiliation, injustice and betrayal. We all carry a main wound among these. It becomes our lens through which we see things. We majorly interpret life's events through the perspective of this wound. We also possess other small wounds among these. They are considered secondary.

To protect ourselves from the sufferings linked to these wounds, our ego has created masks for us. Before going into detail about this, I would like to specify here what I mean by *ego*. The ego is the representation we make of ourselves. It is a personality culminating from our experiences and our memories. It is our inner child who, being a little guardian, has developed strategies to be loved by its parents and to protect itself from suffering. It has constructed itself at the age of two or three, and copes as best it can to make life happier for us. Today, as adults, we can see that it limits us with certain beliefs, provokes fears and dislikes suffering; it gladly represses emotions that seem uncomfortable. This can make our lives tumultuous and punctuated with anxieties. Anxieties manifest themselves when too many emotions have been pushed back and haven't been experienced. However, this ego is to be thanked, as it has done its best to take us across the turbulent period of childhood.

From a spiritual point of view, the ego must be controlled, as by making us wear masks, it distances us from our soul. In liberating ourselves from our ego that we can discover the spiritual awakening – synonymous with connection to the self and unity with the world. It's a wonderful experience, however, we need this ego to live our human experience. We must learn to control it rather than let it control our life. Being conscious of its role, we can realize that some of our little guardian's choices do not suit our adult life anymore. We can re-choose some attitudes whilst thanking it for its reflexes that were necessary for the child we once were. We can see its beliefs that limit us, transform the fears into trust and learn to welcome the emotions that the ego has been so used to pushing away.

Now that we have an understanding of its definition, Lise Bourbeau teaches us that our ego will make us wear a mask to hide our wounds. Like a glove that we slide onto our hand to protect an open wound from dirt, rain or sun, the ego will make us have reactions to avoid the suffering of our painful wounds. This might seem like a good idea at first. The intention is there, but once an adult, the result is chaotic. If someone dares to hold your hand out of love for you, you risk to scream from pain and to run away. These masks are reactions that become character traits, but they are not who we truly are. Thanks to the observation of our behaviours, we can identify these masks that we wear and that hide our wounds.

The wound of rejection makes us wear the mask of the fleer. The fleer doubts their right to exist and is always afraid of disturbing others or taking up too much space. It makes us discrete and we don't want to make waves or disrupt. We avoid conflict, push discussions away and might even reject others to avoid being rejected ourselves. This masks brings us in our own world, our bubble. We are equally detached from the material world and more attracted to the intellectual or spiritual world. We doubt our worth and don't have a lot of confidence in ourselves. We fulfil this with perfectionism, to be sure of having value in the eyes of others. The wound of rejection heals when we start to see ourselves at our true value. We dare to set boundaries and say no. We put our dreams in focus and make our own projects more tangible.

The wound of abandonment makes us wear the mask of the dependent. The dependent has the feeling of not being able to succeed alone and often asks for help from others. We are afraid of solitude and don't like carrying out activities alone or making decisions alone. Since then, we need the approval of others to be able to progress. The dependent's mask is also very emotive and sensitive to other's emotions. We often present ourselves as victims to attract the attention. The wound of abandonment heals when we begin to identify our needs and when we manage to take care of them. By taking the responsibility of our needs into our own hands, we are no longer dependent on others and discover that we can live, happily, in an autonomous way.

The wound of humiliation makes us wear the mask of the masochist. The masochist unconsciously searches pain and humiliation. We behave as such, as we see ourselves as worse than others, without a heart, unworthy of love. We like to feel free, but are afraid of not having boundaries, which would push us into excesses or doing things we wouldn't be proud of. They don't listen to their own needs and give to others what they don't give to themselves. They like to feel useful. The humiliation wound heals when we ask ourselves what our needs are before saying 'yes'. We take on fewer responsibilities and feel much freer.

The wound of betrayal makes us wear the mask of the dominant. The dominant needs to control and dominate others. We can thus present ourselves as bossy and like to have the last say. We ensure that others respect their commitments to avoid feeling betrayed again. We have an active mind, love planning in advance and have difficulties letting go. The wound of betrayal heals when we develop confidence in ourselves, in others and in life. Things rarely happen as planned, but it's good this way. We learn to let go and to simply be, without having to feel different or exceptional.

The wound of injustice makes us wear the mask of rigidity. The rigid cuts us off from our emotions and feelings. We often choose to never love and close off our heart. We are, of course, very sensitive, but present ourselves as cold and strict towards others. The mask of rigidity needs for things to be fair and places a lot of attention on that. We also struggle treating ourselves and feel really guilty when not in action. The wound of injustice heals when we soften and are less perfectionist towards ourselves. We learn to enjoy the little pleasures of life and to express our emotions. We dare to open our hearts and show our sensitivity.

You wonder what your main wound and mask might be? You can download a guide on my website that will take you through a quiz to identify your wounds. It will also give you tips to let go of your masks. Please, feel free to download it here : www.eleonoredeposson.com/freetools

We react in certain ways to situations depending on our primary or secondary wound. In the case of a break up, people with the wound of rejection will feel rejected. They will want to disappear and stay alone in their own corner. Others would feel humiliated and unworthy, and would punish themselves by, for example, eating far too much. A third group would feel betrayed and would maintain perfect control of their life by showing themselves as capable of handling everything. If we are governed by these behaviours, we are in *reaction* and not in action. Our feelings, our actions and our choices are dictated by our mask and not by our higher self. We will react with the part of us that does not want to suffer. Except it suffers anyway.

Our soul faces situations with calmness and care. When we are in alignment with this, we can express ourselves calmly, set our limits, communicate our affection, listen to and satisfy our needs, be fully ourselves whilst feeling free.

You might have recognised yourself in one of the above

descriptions. If that's the case, good, you will be able to identify more easily when you are in reaction and wearing your mask rather than in alignment with yourself. If you did not recognise yourself in these descriptions, are hesitating between several wounds, or are confused, do not worry. It is not necessary to know our wounds in order to heal. We will treat the emotions coming from them and heal them in the next chapter.

Love as healing

> "Love is meant to heal. Love is meant to renew."
> Deepak Chopra[3]

Love is the biggest force, the most beautiful energy in the Universe. It is a healing energy, as lack of love or the illusion of lacking love is the source of the majority of our suffering. This lack of love doesn't necessarily need to have been real. The illusion of it is enough to create a wound. Doctor Leonard Laskow explains very well in the book *Healing with Love,* that it is the experience of separation or the perception of a separation between two human beings – that's to say the perception of a lack of love – that creates a wound.

He teaches that these separations generally take place during childhood or even in the womb.[4] The mother might ask herself if she will manage to take proper care of her child, she worries and is afraid of not being up to the task. The foetus feels this fear. It asks itself how it will survive, as the survival instinct is a human's motor. It thinks that maybe something isn't right with him, a reason why its mother would worry. It will live through a separation between itself and its mother and an emotional wound will appear.

This process is not conscious, but it remains engraved in us and will dictate our reactions. It can also take place when a father wishes to have a son, but it is a girl that sees the day. Or again, with a mother who is cooking a lovely meal and asks her child to wait 5 minutes before serving them a glass of water. All of these events can leave a perception of a lack of love. In terms of wound, they imprint themselves as rejection, abandonment, injustice, betrayal or humiliation.

So, to heal these wounds that have been provoked by a form of separation, or the illusion of a separation, between two human beings, which will be felt as a lack of love, the only true solution is to replace it with love, plenty of love. Self-love above all else.

Loving and accepting ourselves also comes with accepting the experiences we live through. This does not mean that we must relive these experiences, but simply allow ourselves to live them to come out stronger and see what they have brought us. We can thus recognize what is fair and good for us and what is not. This will make us progress in the resolving of our equation.

To conclude, the Self-Healing Circle begins with this first step: "The Wound." It's a step that can be synonymous with realization, but that's not always the case. As already mentioned, it is not necessary to know one's wounds to progress in the healing journey, as they express themselves anyway through the second step: "The Emotion." The wound heals through its succeeding step, the circle's last step: Love. These three steps are inactive steps that we pass through. They are influenced by three active steps: Welcome and Honour, Transmute, Practice. Three verbs that put us into action.

We learn to become the master, the artist of our own life. Of course, this will depend on us. It's us who decide how to lead the dance. It's all about our free will. The School of Life offers a wide range of experiences that we choose to live through or not. We choose everything, starting from our inner world. We can choose to renounce certain events and their lessons, attract them to us, stay blocked, outgrow or overcome them. We have the entire power to decide what we do with this School and how we address it. We can also change our way of addressing it along the way.

This book's humble objective is to provide you with a healing track that stems from my own experience and my own little cloud.

What we have learned from this chapter:

- We all have wounds and gifts. Living, suffering, falling, getting back up, believing and loving is the only way to discover these wounds and gifts.
- Our wounds are born in a lack of love, real or perceived. They heal with love. Self-love, above anything else.
- Our wounds make us wear masks. Reactions provoked by the ego that wishes to protect us from suffering.
- Our reactions, that's to say our emotions, are the visible part of our wounds.
- It is not essential to know one's wound to be able to use the Self-Healing Circle. It helps if that's the

case, but given that the wound will express itself through emotions, we will treat those.

- Make sure to download my guide helping you to let go of your masks :
www.eleonoredeposson.com/freetools

3

STEP 2: THE EMOTION

W hat is an emotion? Where does it come from? Why does it express itself? What purpose does it have? And what to do with our emotions? This chapter will make you discover these uncomfortable sensations, that make us act or react, without always understanding why.

The nature of emotion

Emotion is energy in movement.[1] To understand this, we have to get back into the nature of the body. Our body seems solid. However, if we zoom into our skin 1 million times, we will find ourselves facing an atom. And if we look inside this atom we will see nothing other than emptiness and tiny particles of energy moving at the speed of light. We seem solid but, in reality, we are just Energy. We are composed of energies that travel through us, like sensations or a feeling that we identify as emotions.

The word 'emotion' has its root in the Latin word *emovere*, meaning 'to move'. Emotion is the body's reaction to a stimulus. Its objective is to indicate for us the nature of a situation, whether it's a danger or a suffering, in order to put us into adequate motion. It is the result of an experience.

Several studies contradict each other in establishing the number of basic emotions we have, but they generally agree with each other in citing 6 main ones: Sadness, Fear, Anger, Disgust, Surprise and Happiness. A whole series of secondary emotions is created by mixing these basic emotions, so, shame is a mix of fear and anger. To them, feelings are a declination of our emotions. They are issued from our mind and are not so much a physical reaction in the body as they are an experience. They can occupy our mind for hours whilst emotions are more short-lived.

We generally have a tendency to categorize our emotions as positive or negative. However, in doing so, we emit a judgment of their subject. Emotions are neither good, nor bad, nor positive, nor negative. They are "the sign that our psyche tries to heal itself."[2] They are messengers. I will thus talk about pleasant or unpleasant, comfortable or uncomfortable emotions, as all emotions have their fair place in our head and body. Some are more gentle, others more intense. At the start, they are just physical sensations such as heat, tension or stomach cramps. We follow by naming these feelings and identifying them as emotions: frustration, shame, admiration, interest.

You might be asking yourself why I haven't spoken of joy as a primary emotion. In fact, it is generally associated with the 6 main emotions. Here I'm taking the opposite side by stating that joy is not an emotion. It is a superior state to emotions, that is uniquely reserved for humans. In fact, joy is not secreted from the limbic system, the animal brain creating our emotions. It is issued from our conscience and is the direct consequence of self-love. Joy is spiritual and manifests itself when we are entirely ourselves, in the fulfillment of our gifts and listening to our deepest needs. Joy is happiness in a serene mind.

The origin of emotion

Chiropractor and lecturer Joe Dispenza participated in several studies on the brain's functioning.[3] He teaches that human beings have the capability to create emotions out of events, but also from simple thoughts. If an animal is in danger, it quickly reacts to survive. The response to feeling fear allows it to escape and as soon as the danger disappears, it will continue with its business without the slightest of worry. The reaction is short and provoked by a real event. Humans, on the other hand, can have a short or long emotion, provoked by an event or a thought. We are much more complex, as the brain doesn't know the difference between an experience and a thought or a vision. Whether we imagine a stressful situation or go through a stressful situation, our body reacts in the same way. It increases our cardiac rhythm, accelerates our breathing, makes us hot and we arrive little by little to a certain level of anxiety. Have you ever panicked and imagined the absolute worst? Yes, our thoughts create these emotions.

"Our emotions are created by an event or the imagination of an event."

Our mind is constantly producing thoughts. Several thoughts cross us throughout the day. Are you conscious of everything you think constantly? Do the following exercise: sit calmly for 10 minutes and note all of the thoughts you get. You will see that it passes from a list of errands you need to do before the weekend, to the presentation you could've done better, or a conversation that bothered you. Our mind is constantly creating thoughts and these thoughts create emotions.

If emotions emerge following an event or a thought, there's also something else that makes us react in a different way to our neighbour. Why do we think a situation is unfair whilst another qualifies it as humiliating? Because our ego is the one that will provoke thoughts of humiliation or injustice. As is explained in the preceding chapter, the ego is the sum of our experiences. It makes us react in a certain way with the aim of protecting us from suffering.

As for our wounds and our experiences, we will have a different reaction than someone else facing an identical situation. This makes us perfectly unique, as we have unique wounds and experiences. We are consequently the only ones who possess the key to our own healing. We find this key by listening to our emotions and understanding that they express our needs.

The objective of emotions

If the ego makes us have certain thoughts and these create emotions, these emotions create, in turn, behaviours. In the case of an imminent danger, fear would be a form of intuition that would allow us to flee. Thus, emotions protect us, they help us to survive and face difficulties.

All of our emotions have a common objective: pass through us. Once an emotion has been entirely experienced, it disappears. Emotions just pass through. They give room to relief once they have been able to express themselves through our body. However, we are often afraid of our own emotions and we don't know what to do with them. We don't want to live through the uncomfortable emotion that is emerging. We have the feeling that it will invade us, that we will lose control and that the pain will be unbearable. We have a feeling of insecurity when we fight against the sadness that invades us and we avoid going within. Yet, the best way to feel safe is in fact by experiencing this sadness, letting it pass through us and seeing that everything is ok. Our emotions exist for our own good. They pass through, help us release what's necessary and then leave.

Doctor Joe Dispenza teaches us that if we don't welcome emotions as soon as they arrive, they then become our identity. In fact, if we experience anger for a prolonged period after an event, it turns little by little into a mood, then a personality trait before becoming part of our identity. Our body stays in the emotion of anger. The simple fact of rethinking about it provokes a new anger and after a few weeks, months or years, we don't know anymore why everything annoys us. Anger becomes our first reaction to everything. This becomes our identity, to the point where the body searches stimuli to react again with anger, given that we "are angry". How long do you wish to feel this anger for? I'll respond for you: as long as you wish to have a child experience this pain. So, simply let it pass through you. It knows which entrance to knock on, and does so for as long as it hasn't done its job. It will then find the exit door of your body and your heart.

> **"If you can communicate with your emotions with empathy while considering them as the bright messengers they are, then you will have all of the energy and information you need to live a meaningful and conscious life."**
> **Karla Mclaren[4]**

Emotions also have an individual objective of their own. They each have their raison d'être. Karla McLaren, American empath and author, shares in her fascinating book *The*

Language of Emotions, that our emotions are, in reality, tools of healing and they each have a mission. Here are the main emotions and their purpose :

Sadness has the mission of regenerating us. It makes tears stream down and leave us calmer so that our body can evacuate what is necessary. I have observed that it grounds us and relaxes us deeply. It allows us to let go of muscular tensions, hopes and disappointments. It liberates us from what no longer serves us. This cleanse leaves room to regeneration. We often feel tired after crying, precisely because the body is repairing itself. This is why sadness often hides behind other emotions, given that it then allows the body to evacuate them. Sadness is healing so never hold back your tears, but surrender yourself to them. Thank them for helping you heal.

Anger is a form of protection. It appears when we feel that we should set our limits or that we have a deep interest in a situation. In fact, we make ourselves angry for things that are really important to us. Anger is proportional to our interest; we don't get angry when something has not significance for us. Anger is to be honoured, as it protects us, helps us to set limits. If, however, it transforms into rage and controls us regularly, it would perhaps be helpful to direct ourselves to a doctor or therapist to understand what is happening inside of us. These moments of crisis are exhausting for the body and the brain and we will need a frame to welcome judiciously the anger that tries to protect us.

Disgust is the total rejection of a behaviour or an object. Karla McLaren explains that it is associated to a type of hate and its objective is also to protect us given that hate is a concentration of anger. When we express our disgust for something or someone, in reality, we project on them our dark sides. This rejection of a behaviour or undesired object that finds itself in us, offers us an immense relief. When we welcome our own disgust, we reconstruct immediately our boundaries and evolve by cleansing ourselves of these undesired objects.

Happiness is an ensemble of gaiety, fun, anticipation and hope. It is a magnificent emotion, but also the most dangerous, as we often look for it without really knowing where to find it, yet it's often right in front of us. Like the other emotions, happiness comes when it decides to, not when we book it in. When it's here, we can welcome it by laughing, smiling and dreaming. We can allow ourselves to be happy for a moment and let it pass, like all other emotions. Its objective is to celebrate our life and to congratulate us.

Fear is not synonymous with worry, anxiety, terror or panic. Karla McLaren teaches us that we easily confuse fear with these three states. In reality, fear, in its natural and spontaneous state, is synonymous with intuition and action. It makes us alert. It makes our mind sharp and ready to react quickly. It brings us into the present moment. It comes to save us from danger when it presents itself. We need to relearn to identify fear as it is. For example, when we are driving and glance at the rearview mirror to see if we can change direction. In this moment, our fear is in its natural state. It is intuitive and will put us into action.

While we ignore the intuition that represents this fear, we leave room for panic, as we no longer feel safe. We don't listen to the instinct that keeps us safe anymore. We can thus experience one of three following types of fear. When they emerge, it is impossible for us to move forward, as they paralyze us. They are identified in the same way by our nervous system though they are not of the same nature.

Knowing them allows us to identify them in our lives when we experience them. The first fear is considered natural fear and it is the real fear Karla McLaren describes. The two following will here be considered "fears", but don't forget that they are in reality synonymous of "intuition".

- Natural Fear

This fear is created by a real danger. Our survival instinct informs us that there is a danger and that we must react very quickly. It presents itself in a fast and intuitive way. This indispensable fear comes to our reptilian brain. It finds itself in the middle of the head and descends the spinal cord. This part of the brain runs other animalistic emotions such as dominations, power or control.

- "Fear" of the Unknown

This fear manifests itself as soon as we leave our comfort zone. It is profoundly rooted in us, as it comes from our ancestors. They dread the world outside their cave, as it was filled with dangers. It's impossible to see this fear disappear, as it is part of us. However, we can learn to control and analyze the situation each time it presents itself to verify if there is a real danger or not. The most successful people are those who experience fear more often, but who manage to control their fear of the unknown. The success finds itself outside of the comfort zone.

- "Fear" of Future Probabilities

This fear survives when we imagine "what might happen if..." This fear is passed on judgments, beliefs, and negative thoughts. It is controllable and can even disappear if we don't maintain it. It limits us uselessly and is to be banished.

Coach Salvica Bogdanov creates a lovely parallel between fears and monsters that hide under our beds as kids: they disappear when we shed light on them.[5] When children are afraid of monsters hiding under their beds and prevent them from sleeping, they go to their parents to ask for help. They enter the room, switch on the light and look under the bed to show their children that there's nothing under the bed. The monster disappeared as soon as the light switched on. The same thing happens with our fears, mainly the fear of the unknown and future possibilities. When we shed light on them, they dissipate and disappear quickly. To place them in the light, all you need to do is to simply express them.

Personal Story: I'm afraid

The day after signing my divorce, life placed a man on my path. Given that my heart was wounded and frightened, I wasn't ready to commit to any sort of thing. I simply had no interest in it, as I wanted to reconstruct myself alone. He lived in Vancouver and was spending several weeks in London. Living in Belgium, it thus seemed obvious to me that us meeting committed me to nothing. It would simply help me to regain confidence in myself. A few days after having met, he told me he wanted to see me again. He organized to come to Brussels one week later. He planned to stay for five days. As we both worked, we would only spend our evenings together and slowly get to know each other. Like any wild start, we showed ourselves in the best light possible, had butterflies in our stomachs, laughed a lot and made the most of the present moment. I wasn't opening much. I kept a lot of things to myself and thought it was the best tactic to protect myself. I didn't want to fall for this guy who was going back to Canada a few weeks later.

At the end of the five days, I had to admit that we had gotten really close. We had discovered a ton of things in common and had spent a week of lovely moments. At this stage, I thought I was still protected by my funny, young lady mask, and didn't feel attached to him. Even if he pleased me, I had no expectations. After his departure, today's technology allowed us to keep in touch daily. He quickly suggested that we see each other again. He had work trips coming up, but wanted to come back to Belgium. Four weeks later, here he would be again, for 10 days this time.

Three days before his arrival, I started to panic. I didn't know what I wanted. I liked him a lot, but I didn't see the point in spending ten days together if he would be flying to the other side of the world anyway. I didn't want a relationship, even less a long-distance relationship. But maybe the distance would give me the time and space that I needed? I didn't want to *not* see him either. I was afraid to be with him, I was afraid not to be with him. What if my heart got broken again? After all, everything has an end! I was a flayed, sensitive little nestling. But it was too late. He had already bought his tickets and repeated every day that he couldn't wait to see me. I would rationalize by telling myself: *it'll be 10 days of fun and that's it. I take what life is offering me.* It was all very well to be rationalizing; the fear came back every day. Every time it knocked at the door, I banned it from coming inside, repeating: *it's ten days of fun and that's it!*

He finally arrives and I put my mask back on. With a smile on my face and a relaxed appearance, I had a wonderful first night. The next morning, when alone in the kitchen, I completely crack. The fear comes back accompanied by tears this time. *What if I fall in love with him and he doesn't want me anymore? And what if he falls in love with me? I'm not ready! I don't want a relationship. I don't know what I want. I'm too scared to have my heart hurt. I don't want to be with him, well yes... maybe?* The tears ran down from my frightened eyes without stopping. I'm completely paralyzed. I panic and dwell on these thoughts for a good half hour. Then, I manage to get a grip and continue with my day as if nothing had happened. He has no idea about the state of panic I have been finding myself in for several days.

By the end of the fourth day, I'm starting to admit that it can't go on. I'm ruining everything. I decide to talk to him in the evening, after our respective days of work. We had planned to join our mutual friends through whom we'd met. This will lighten the mood between us if the conversation doesn't go well. I'm afraid that he won't understand. I don't know how he will react. I'm not even sure what I'll tell him.

It's 7.30pm. I'm ready and we need to leave in 30 minutes. This gives me the time to share with him what I've been hiding for over a week now. I sit cross-legged on the bed and suggest that he does the same because I want to talk to him. He's a bit surprised, looks at me, intrigued, and sits in front of me. I take all my courage and start. There's a knot in my throat:

I would like to share something with you. I've been trying to understand what I've been feeling but it's not really working. I'm gonna try to find the right words to express this and I would like you to listen first.

My voice trembles and tears are surging.

Since you arrived, when I'm alone in the day, I cry. I cry because I'm afraid. My heart has been broken and my body has registered that love hurts.

Tears are running down.

I don't know what we are. We have never discussed what we are. We have never established our situation given that you are soon leaving to Canada and it seemed complicated for what follows.

However, I spend my time trying to see signs, to understand if we are a couple or not. When you talk to a girl, I surprise myself thinking that you'll think she's prettier than me and that it's over. When you compliment me, it reassures me, but then I panic. I'm afraid of being in a relationship with you. I'm afraid of a long-distance relationship. I'm afraid of getting hurt. I'm afraid of not being with you. I'm afraid of never seeing you again. Basically, I'm afraid of everything. It paral-

yses me and I'm not able to make the most of your presence here.

All of this really means that I'm attached to you, when I thought of protecting myself and living in the present moment, without expectations. I don't know what I want and I think that I, above all, need to reconstruct myself. I should probably do this alone. My priority at the moment, is me.

His hands placed on my knees, he looks at me straight in the eyes with so much gentleness, then lowers his gaze to prepare his response. A moment passes. He thanks for me being honest and having shared all these feelings with me. He responds that he understands, that the priority is that I first reconstruct myself. Given that he's soon to leave, he doesn't have a response to give me regarding whether or not we're a couple, but he will think about it. He wasn't thinking given the uncertain future and was enjoying the present moment. He continues by adding that he appreciates all the moments we spend together, that he's happy that I opened up to him today, because he too is attached to me. His response makes me smile. He dries the tears on my cheeks. I feel relieved. An immense weight was just lifted from my shoulders. I finally breathe.

This story presents to you fears as little monsters. They leave the day we finally dare to put them in the spotlight. In reality, this goes for all emotions. Expressing them, sharing them with authenticity is one of the easiest ways to see them fly away immediately.

.   .   .

Emotions stock up. They are a recording of the past.

When an event takes place in our life, a long process engages. If it's one that isn't perceived as happy, it will come to revive one of our wounds. Thoughts will emerge, they create emotions, and those emotions create behaviours. If the emotion is too strong or is suppressed, the body stores it to allow us to digest it in several goes. The emotion that we experience in the future will actually be a recording of the past. Emotions are the trace of a past experience and of its respective unexpressed emotion. This can happen in several ways.

In the case of a recent event, we can become aware of a suppressed emotion and give it the opportunity to free itself later in the day or week. We can learn to go within, give space to what must be expressed, welcome it and let it circulate so that it can then leave. What we experience in this moment is, in reality, the trace of a recent experience that didn't have the opportunity to express itself yet. Thanks to our intervention, the emotion can be liberated quickly.

In the event of a suppressed emotion, a similar event, or not, will allow us to free the weight of that past experience. We are likely to have an excessive reaction regarding the actual situation, given that the stored emotion will be linked to the past, but not to the present. But in the end, the stored emotion will be partially or entirely freed thanks to the actual event.

When the emotion isn't welcomed at all, it will place itself in certain parts of the body, coming out in the form of physical suffering. The stored emotion gradually damages our organs and expresses itself in the form of illnesses such as chronic fatigue, digestive problems, back pain, depression, etc. Malady is the physical representation of an emotional disharmony inside us. The French phrase 'le mal a dit' [the pain has said] shows us that malady comes to inform us of something. Quebec psychotherapist Jacques Martel dedicated part of his career to putting together a book sharing the message of each illness.[6] Our sicknesses have something to tell us. They don't happen *to* us, they happen *for* us.

When the emotion is far too strong to be experienced in one go, we might also enter a state of emotional shock. The stress experienced is so intense that the brain must react for our own survival. It will engage a process of dissociation, as an emotional storm like in the loss of a loved one, a sudden breakup , physical violence, can represent a life risk for the organism. In fact, the excess of adrenaline and cortisol puts the heart and brain in danger. And so will begin a neurobiological mechanism that will disjoint the emotional circuit in order to produce an emotional anesthesia. We don't feel anything. It is impossible to express an emotion while thinking about the relevant event. The dissociation produces itself just after the event or in the hours that follow. It can be light or intense and will last, in accordance with this, several days, weeks or months. If you have already gone through this experience, you will recognize yourself in the fact that you feel like a stranger to the situation. You are the spectator of your own life. You feel nothing. This subconscious survival reflex is rather impressive. It can even go further and cut connections with the hippocampus, the part of the brain that guides the memory. This is why certain people have a memory lapse with regards to the time of the shock. This unconscious memory is called the traumatic memory. It comes back in the form of flashbacks, panic attacks or nightmares. In this case, deep work with a psychiatrist or other emotion-related professionals is necessary to bring the memory of the subconscious back to the conscious and allow it to be released in a safe and compassionate environment.

Suppressed emotions always return to allow us to let go of the weight of the past. They are like luggages, which we will drag along until we give them the space they deserve. However, they can also become the key of our own interior treasures if we know how to welcome them. Whether it's an emotional shock or a suppressed frustration, we can master them and overcome them to avoid them becoming a mood, a character trait or a personality. When we know that our emotions are a form of programming, we can decide to control our emotions rather than letting them control us. This mastering suggests welcoming, honouring and letting go. The Self-Healing Spiral allows this.

Personal Story: Rejected or Loved?

This reminds me of a situation where I felt wounded and rejected, even though the young man in front of me was telling me that I was his everything. Absurd, right? The relationship of which I spoke about a few pages earlier had taken root. We had finally decided to give ourselves a chance, despite the distance. A while later, when love began to birth, he wanted to be sure that our relationship had a good foundation by being honest. He knew that trust and honesty were primordial to me, given my history. He thus took his courage in his hands and announced the following: before spending the summer in Europe, he was seeing a girl in Vancouver, where he lived. They were not a couple, but spent time together. The North-American custom of 'dating'. The moment he would return to Canada, the relationship would continue from where it left off prior to his departure to Europe. Between those times, they weren't talking to each other.

After having met me, he pushed back his return several times, as he wished to see me again. He lived in London and planned to come see me in Brussels twice. Once he realized that he had feelings for me, he told the girl that he had met someone else and that put an end to their ambiguity. He shared this story with me because he wanted to really construct something with me and it seemed important to him to start on a healthy and honest foot, even if I could've never heard of this story. In his eyes, I was the only person he thought of everyday and for whom he had sincere feelings.

When he finished telling me this story, I had just one desire: to cry. *Why was he talking about someone else? This girl was surely important to him if he was talking about her! Why hide her? He'll surely do the same thing to me!* I felt so rejected and betrayed. I didn't understand why someone else was appearing in our story. It didn't make any sense.

I went outside to get some fresh air and have a few minutes alone. Tears inevitably ran down my cheeks. I felt like I had lost him. Then, my intellect came to the surface and said: he just told you that you were the only person he has feelings for and that he wants to build something with you. Why do you feel rejected and betrayed? On this day, I realised that my body had stayed in the past. The sadness, rejection and betrayal that occupied my entire being were linked to a past experience. I was reliving the moment where my ex-husband was telling me about another young woman and announcing that he loved her and was leaving me for her, six months after marrying me.

My ego, in order to protect me, was making me feel rejected and betrayed so that I would distance myself from him and even consider a breakup. On the other hand, my intellect sincerely understood his approach: he wanted to develop a serious relationship on an honest foundation without secrets and with trust. I found myself battling between my body and my head. Who was right? Who should I follow? My emotions seemed justified: I thought I had the right to feel rejected and betrayed, but in reality, they weren't so justified, as he just wanted to commit to me. My emotions belonged to a past event and resurged to protect me, but weren't adequate. Rather than letting myself be over-whelmed by my feelings of sadness and rejection, which would have provoked a stormy discussion and could've pushed me to kick him out – reject the other before being rejected yourself – I let my emotions pass through me to liberate myself from them. Then, I took a step back, breathed deeply and chose a second emotion to face the situation.

I came back into the room and shared with him the battle that created several emotions in me, rejection and sadness, but also gratitude and hope. Yes, I felt gratitude towards his honesty and hope for this relationship that would grow from honest foundations. I didn't let my emotions control me, but mastered them to then choose more constructive and appropriate emotions to express.

· · ·

Our emotions act like two-way radios

American author Don Tulman explains that our emotions, which are energy in movement, act on the level of our subconscious like transmitters and receivers. We attract what we feel.

If we are terribly afraid that we'll get in an accident, it will happen: from a mental point of view, we will concentrate our attention on the accident and from an energetic point of view, we will attract the energy that we feel towards us. Our emotions create emotional models that provoke repetitive situations. These models are provoked by our beliefs and influence all of our relationships, whether they are personal, professional, our relationship with money, etc. Haven't you ever found yourself in repetitive situations? Been sacked several times in a row? Always falling for married men? Falling in love with people who don't want to commit? Always lacking money at the end of the month?

These repetitive situations are generally increasingly stronger to open our eyes and show us that there's a problem. The concept is simple: don't expect a different result if you're always doing the same thing. However, if you change your attitude and your thoughts, you will quickly increase your chances of experiencing a different situation. The good news is that it's possible to increase our comfortable emotions. When 'abandoned', the brain will always focus on what isn't right. Our natural thoughts are negative, but we can train ourselves to have positive thoughts that, in turn, create pleasant emotions. As a muscle, our brain will reinforce itself and the neural pathways of comfortable emotions will be myelinated to give us quicker access to joy, enthusiasm, adventure, opportunity. Whilst fear, anger and frustration show themselves as toxic by freeing stress hormones, comfortable emotions are necessary to reestablish balance in our mind.

Emotion is a knock on our door

Emotions have a purpose. Let this sink... Emotions have a purpose. They teach us things about ourselves and make us live experiences we need in order to progress. They make us grow and evolve, which is our primary objective. Life is made to be experienced and it presents us experiences bringing up necessary emotions for our evolution. We attract these events given that our emotions act as transmitters and receivers.

When we open the door at the first knock, the emotion enters smoothly and dissipates after a good conversation. Imagine that it simply wants to come have a cup of tea with you. It has something to tell you and it is important for the emotion to talk about it with you. It will stay, waiting, at your entrance door and will knock every now and then until you open to her and listen. Yes, emotions are stubborn. But it's for our own good.

Emotions allow us to progress on the healing path. It is for this reason that unwelcomed emotions can occupy our mind for an entire day. They continue to knock at the door. Here is a lovely poem, *The Guest House,* by the writer Rumi, that illustrates this marvelously:

> *This being human is a guest house.*
> *Every morning a new arrival.*
> *A joy, a depression, a meanness,*
> *some momentary awareness comes*
> *as an unexpected visitor.*
> *Welcome and entertain them all!*
> *Even if they're a crowd of sorrows,*
> *who violently sweep your house*
> *empty of its furniture,*
> *still, treat each guest honourably.*
> *He may be clearing you out*
> *for some new delight.*
> *The dark thought, the shame, the malice,*
> *meet them at the door laughing,*
> *and invite them in.*
> *Be grateful for whoever comes,*
> *because each has been sent*
> *as a guide from beyond.*

In the following chapter I explain how to open the door to one's emotions and allow them to live. I will share concrete tools with you so that you can welcome and honour your emotions as they deserve. We will enter the active steps of the Self-Healing Circle.

. . .

In the meantime, here are the main concepts we have learned in this chapter:

- Emotions are traces of the past. They are an endproduct of a past experience, like Dr Joe Dispenza teaches it.
- Emotions can be provoked by an event or a thought.
- Emotions that aren't welcomed become a mood, character trait, personality and finally our identity. Our brain will then search for ways to make us relive this emotion (anger, frustration etc.) given that it is our identity.
- Emotions knock at the door of our heart for as long as we don't open the door to them. Let them pass through you, they will leave just as soon.
- Emotions are our allies. They help us to discover who we are and the needs we have.

STEP 3: WELCOME & HONOUR

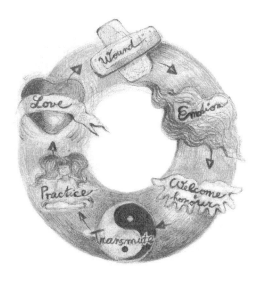

"Welcome your emotion". You have no idea how many times I heard this. Every therapist that I met during my divorce repeated this same phrase. One in particular added, "you need to experience your emotions, otherwise they will come back. Wholly embrace your sadness, you don't have a choice." I thought I was experiencing the sadness every day, but apparently, I wasn't doing it very well. It's true, I had no idea how to do. I didn't know what it really meant. I hated feeling that discomfort twisting my stomach. I wasn't welcoming my sadness, I was suppressing it constantly right up until the day of the alarm signal: the first panic attack. It took me a few days to understand that this panic attack was the result of too many suppressed emotions. I was going to have to learn to welcome what was happening within me. I was going to have to feel all of this discomfort and I was terrified. I took one step at a time, until the day I understood that welcoming my emotions, was relieving. I understood that emotions have a *raison d'être*. They have a message to deliver and that's why they come knocking at our door. The third step in the Self-Healing Spiral will teach us how to open the door to them. It's the first active step where you enter in the game. You will discover how to welcome and honour your emotions. Daring to simply feel them.

Suppressing the emotion

When an emotion passes through us, it can have the effect of a little wave like that of a tsunami. Depending on the situation and the depth of the wound, we will need to face several waves. We might start by feeling our stomach twist, shivers going through us, warmth rising, cheeks reddening... Different physical expressions will come to the surface to signal that something on the inside needs to circulate. What do we usually do in this situation? We have a tendency to suppress these sensations hoping that they are going to disappear. It's typical and I did it for years. I was too afraid of looking ridiculous where I simply wanted to be Miss Perfect. Our society doesn't give much room for emotions. In its eyes, crying is synonymous with weakness. So, when an emotion arrives, whether we are alone or surrounded, we know a ton of tricks to continue as if nothing was wrong. We continue talking with our voice trembling, we change the subject, we block our breathing and fall into survival mode where we are quiet and close ourselves up entirely to all dialogue. Rarely do we take the time to breathe deeply to give the fair space to what is happening inside of us. Rarely do we close our eyes and give space to silence to feel the height of the wave that encircles us.

When we suppress our emotions, we send them back inside us, hoping to see them evaporate. Unfortunately, this is not how it works. They have precisely come from this inner world and choose to express themselves in a particular moment to free us. If not welcomed, they will come back. Suppressed emotions always come back. They even manifest themselves more intensely to ensure that they get our attention. If we send them back again, they end up by transforming themselves. Fear and anger can present themselves as tics, compulsions, psychosomatic illnesses, addictions or neuroses. Suppressing our emotions is actually quite a dangerous way to manage them.

Let us illustrate this with an example: in a meeting, your boss talks about a project on which you have worked immensely and it has been met with great success. However, he doesn't cite you and praises himself for your work. He shares the information that you collected and pulls the ground from under your feet, assuring that he is congratulated instead of you. You are in shock and don't dare to intervene. You are too afraid of looking ridiculous. You are facing a great injustice, but you can't do anything. You're bubbling inside. The meeting finishes. His bosses congratulate him again and you leave the room, sick. You throw yourself into your work to take your mind off it. Your anger makes you efficient. You don't say a word to anyone, because it wouldn't change anything anyway and you continue with your day the way it started. The lid covering the boiling saucepan gets you through the day. You did not leave room for the anger, the frustration, the feeling of injustice or rejection. You are particularly tense. Your muscles are tight, your mood is grumpy, and your speech is nonexistent. The negative thoughts don't leave you alone. They stay present in a corner of your head while you work non-stop.

"We suppress our emotions because we don't know what to do with them. We're afraid."

I think you got it. In this case, you have chosen to suppress your emotions. The result? You are the only one undergoing the consequences of the situation; grumpy mood, physical pain... Furthermore, these uncomfortable emotions aren't passing through and stay vivid throughout the day. It'll take you a few glasses of wine or a long jog to think of something else. Maybe you'll fall asleep in a bad mood and will wake up in the same bad mood after sleeping badly. At the end of the day, you undergo unexpressed emotions and don't know anymore why you're in a bad mood. In conclusion, no good comes out of this situation. On the contrary, you accumulate uncomfortable emotions that store in your body and can come back in the form of anxieties. Sooner or later, you will have to leave the space for these emotions if you don't want them to control your life. Suppressing emotions can appear to be a solution, but it's not, even short-term.

We suppress our emotions because we don't know what to do with them. Because we don't know how to let them express themselves nor what purpose it would serve. Because we're afraid of how others see us. Because we have learned, as children, that it's better to be quiet, not to cry, not to get angry, etc. Facing them, numerous people, including myself, could try using the mind to calm down. They would thus try to rationalize the situation. They would find reasons that explain the behaviour of the person that hurt them. These explanations could satisfy the intellect, but won't erase the frustration, the anger, the disgust, the deception. Emotions are experienced like emotions, not like factual elements. The mind can make us take a step back to understand a situation and re-choose the emotion with which we want to face it, but the first emotion on the surface must always be welcomed like a valuable emotion. It has its own place.

Letting yourself be submerged

The second choice that is offered to you is to let yourself be invaded by the emotion. Let's retake the example of the boss needing recognition, reaping the fruits of your labor. You could react in the meeting by manifesting your anger and the injustice of the situation. You could leave the meeting abruptly. You could also make sharp remarks to him during the rest of the meeting. You could also be quiet, then go to the toilet wanting to smash the door. All of these attitudes would have been possible if you had chosen to let yourself be submerged in the emotion.

The emotion would have controlled you and the excessive reaction, though justifiable, could have been badly perceived by your work environment. Would you feel better afterwards? That is unlikely, as your reaction would probably have had detrimental consequences. However, your attitude would have been entirely justified given that your work wasn't valued fairly and the attitude of such a boss isn't appreciated.

Expressing one's emotions while being submerged in them can provoke storms on just as much on the outside as on the inside of us. We can exclaim "You made me angry! You made me cry! It's all your fault!". We then give the power to control our emotions to others. We wound the other and find ourselves completely distressed. This might relieve us for a moment, we have evacuated our anger, but a few minutes later, the internal torment takes place. We feel bad to have lost our temper, or disappointed by our relational competences. Moreover, our brain registers our way of getting annoyed and prepares itself to repeat the same reaction in a future situation. The learning capacities of the brain don't only apply to the learning of a new language or new competences, but also to our way of managing our emotions.. Yes, you might want to pay attention to your reactions.

Finally, it's *you* who chooses what to do with this rising anger. You can suppress it and suffer alone. You can be submerged in it and face other uncomfortable consequences. Or you can choose to welcome the emotion in the given moment and leave the incident behind you.

Welcoming your emotion

Welcoming our emotions means giving them their fair space. Welcomed emotions open doors to our inner world, as they give us a message about ourselves. These treasures are part of the knowledge and understanding of ourselves. Our first mission as human beings is to learn to know ourselves, to heal, to develop our gifts and love ourselves. Emotions are better as allies in this quest.

It is also interesting to remember here that it's our ego provoking our emotions, rather than the person in front of us. We are emotionally programmed to feel uncomfortable emotions in certain situations. We can learn to take a step back and recognize what's provoking the reaction inside us. We can also recognize that the other person has its own wounds pushing them to act in such a way. There is no good or evil on Earth. There are only people who suffer. However, it can turn out to be useful to express ourselves constructively to be respected and place boundaries. After all, we are merely human beings and will appreciate being understood.

So, how could our fictive character react to give a fair

space to their emotions? First of all, he could have started by identifying what he was feeling. What is the main emotion inhabiting in him? Anger, frustration, feelings of injustice, rejection, not being valued? If our character has welcomed and identified his emotion, and he does not agree with what just happened, he can go to his boss after the meeting to share his disagreement. In a state of constructive and calm mind, the following conversation could have taken place:

"Hi Kevin, I would like to talk with you for 5 minutes, if that's ok."

"Yes of course, I'm all yours."

"This morning, when I wasn't cited in the meeting, I didn't feel valued. When this happens, I don't feel like I belong. As I had spent many hours on this project, I was hoping to receive recognition for the fruits of my labour."

Communicating one's emotions authentically is one tool in this step. If we choose to share our feelings with the person who triggered this emotion in us, it is important to talk with the "I" rather than the "you". In fact, approaching the situation in the second person will be perceived as a form of accusation. This will aggravate the situation, as the person in front of you will feel attacked. And the best defense being an attack, they will then attack in return.

Imagine the same conversation in the second person:

"You didn't cite me in the meeting this morning and that's not fair. You reaped the fruits of my labor though you did nothing. You know that I worked enormously on this project and yet you didn't cite me. You don't give me the place that I deserve in this team and that doesn't work for me."

Do you feel the difference? The content of the message is identical, but the form is entirely different. Rather than transmitting one's feelings and talking about one's own point of view, our fictive character will, in a way, accuse the other and underline that his behaviour displeased him. The tone used will be more aggressive and the interlocutor, feeling attacked, will attack in return. A true cockfight will begin. This won't end as much as hoped and might even fire back against our fictive character.

Expressing oneself genuinely is the best way to strengthen a relationship. Often, we are afraid of losing the other if we express ourselves. We are afraid to show our vulnerability and hide it behind a smile. But, being true is the best way to get closer to the other. We gain everything from being true and authentic: relief first, then self-respect and certainly the attention and listening of the other. When we open ourselves to someone, they open as well. We build a relationship of trust. Whether it's a professional relationship, friendship, familial or romantic, sharing our emotions with sincerity and authenticity is essential. Gabrielle, Bernstein, the American lecturer, shares humorously that:

"There is nothing sexier than my authentic truth."[1]
Gabrielle Bernstein

Honouring your emotion

When we honour our emotion, we are more able to offer it the place it deserves rather than fear it. To honour it is to unroll the red carpet for it. It's listening to what it has to say. It's thanking it, as by coming to the surface, it heals us and delivers a message. Emotions are not evil, quite the opposite, they are necessary for our survival and we need them for our fulfillment. When we honour our emotions, we don't suppress them, but seek to live at peace with them. In expressing themselves through our whole body, they liberate us from a weight of the past and bring us closer to healing. Our emotions take care of us and that's why we must honour them and learn to welcome them in the best way possible.

"Honouring one's emotion is taking back one's power"

Once the emotion is put in the spotlight, you can discover the message that it brings: you have unresolved needs, unheard hopes, or unhealed wounds? What's the message? Go within yourself and a voice will end up bringing you the answer. Do you need more emotional security? Attention? Approval? More presence, because you can't stand solitude? I have experienced all of these needs. I thought I had managed to resolve all of this by surrounding myself and attracting attention, until I understood that it changed nothing. I didn't feel good when I was alone with myself. That's when I inverted the tendency to cultivate this love coming from the inside by honouring my emotions. Find your power and don't let the attitude of others dictate your emotions. Welcome them, honour them, as they will make you discover who you are. Then little by little, you will learn to master them with acceptance and surrender.

Finally, this step will develop your emotional intelligence. Emotional intelligence is the ability to identify and manage all your emotions whether they are comfortable or uncomfortable. It quickly assesses the emotion felt and helps you taking a step back. As a muscle, it develops and allows you to act consciously instead of *reacting* in a delicate situation. Emotional intelligence is a form of intelligence being increasingly put forward in our world of permanent communication. In the professional world as well as in our private environment, it offers competences such as self awareness, managing work, empathy, listening and motivation. It neatly influences relationships and collaboration. So, cultivate it by learning to juggle these tools that will help you identify and manage your emotions. Your life will only be lighter with it.

The first tool to welcome and honour your emotions is expressing yourself to the concerned person. There are two others: talking to yourself and writing. You can use just one or each of them. Read them, familiarize yourself with them, and find the one that resonates the most with you. Choose the one that you're most comfortable with. From today, as soon as a daily event affects you, try one of these tools and observe how you feel after applying it. Then, you can choose the one that is most convenient for you or apply them all!

Tool 1.1: Expressing yourself to the concerned person

Expressing what we feel is always very liberating and allows us to share our needs and expectations. The person in front of us isn't always aware of them. Evidently, expressing ourselves to the concerned person is only possible in the case where an emotion is linked to a relationship between two individuals. The person in front of you lives in its own world, with its vision of things, its wounds, its glasses, so it is important to approach this discussion in a healthy and constructive way.

To do so, we will use non-violent communication and its four steps. This methodology features the OFNR model:

Observation, Feelings, Needs and Requests. It originates in the research of Dr Rosenberg, a French psychologist in the 1960s. According to him, all communication becomes more fluid when each person knows what the other needs. The interpretation and form of a communicated message become secondary once we understand the need of our interlocutor. The judgment and criticism are replaced by the understanding of a need looking for satisfaction.

Step 1: Preparing myself

A few tips for the exchange to run well:

- Show proof of authenticity. Be real. Say what's in your heart.
- Only speak in the way that you feel things. Speak from the perspective of "I".
- Don't make accusations. Replace judgment and critique with openness and sincerity.
- Train yourself in advance. Sometimes, we can be taken away by our emotions in a discussion.

Step 2: Write your approach in 4 steps

Set yourself up in a calm place with paper and a pen. Write what you feel by starting with sharing your observation, feeling, need and then your request.

1. Observation: I say what I observe, notice, hear, imagine. Use the keyword *when* to start your sentence.
2. Feeling: I express my emotion or the feeling regarding what I just observed. Continue with *I feel...*
3. Need: I express the need that I have and that is

linked to my feeling or my values. Continue with *because...*

4. Request: I request which actions I would like to see take place.

5. When I don't hear anything from you though we planned to see each other,

6. I feel sad. I feel like you have better things to do,

7. Because I need to feel that our friendship matters to you,

8. I ask you to keep me in the loop if your plans change and you're no longer available.

Step 3: Express yourself to the right person

Go calmly to the person and ask them if they can spare you a few minutes.

If you don't wish to express yourself first hand or don't have the opportunity, you can write to them an email or message following those four steps. Then, they will understand your needs and hopes without feeling attacked. They will be able to act differently in the future and the situation shouldn't happen again.

Tool 1.2: Talking to yourself

The second tool involves talking to yourself, that's to say coming into contact with your inner child. When an emotion emerges, that's where it comes from: our ego, our little guardian, our inner child. So to give him the opportunity to express himself, to deliver his message and give him all the legitimacy he needs, we need to dare going inside ourselves and understand that the emotion is just passing through us.

Imagine a child crying because he lost his toy. If you say to him, "Stop crying and get over it. It's just a toy!" he will cry even harder. Whereas if you say gently, "Why are you sad? Is it because you lost your toy? I understand that you're sad, it's not great losing something we love." He will calm down quickly, feel understood, accepted and listened to. Do the same for yourself. There's no reason to be harsher on yourself than with a child. Hold on and read this again: There's no reason to be harsher on yourself than with a child.

This tool helps you connecting with your inner child, with whom you talk and to whom you give legitimacy. Our wounds appear during our childhood (see Chapter 2) so it's to him/her that we must address ourselves. If you visualize an event that's happened to you as an adult, like in our previous example, you can also address this adult and see him in the same moment from where the event occurred. However, this event will be the result of an unfixed wound from the past, so ideally address yourself to yourself between the ages of 2 and 7. By applying this exercise, you give the possibility to your inner child to express itself in a compassionate environment, free from judgment.

I would equally like to lift all worry regarding emotions that seem unmanageable and invasive. They often seem gigantic to us, precisely because we don't open the door to them. It's our little guardian who is afraid, and doesn't want us to go down to where it hurts. He thinks we're not capable of managing this suffering. Therefor, we don't feel capable of welcoming our emotions. However, embracing them and feeling them is the best way to let them pass through us and to feel safe with them. Don't be afraid. The emotion is your ally and you will gradually feel safe when you're used to welcome your emotions and talking to yourself. The more you practise this exercise, the easier it will seem. I promise.

Step 1: Preparing myself

Sit comfortably in a chair or lay down on your bed. Choose a calm space where you won't be interrupted. You can choose to let the silence surround you or listen to soft, calm, or sad music that will eventually help you go within.

Breathe deeply and think of a precise situation where you felt affected. Show kindness towards yourself. Be the ideal parent to this inner child that needs to be listened to.

Step 2: What do I feel?

How do I feel?

What are the thoughts going through me?

What's affecting me?

Let your thoughts express themselves without trying to control them.

Step 3: How does the emotion expresses itself physically?

1. Observe your body.

What are the feelings that inhabit you?

Do you feel blocked, paralyzed?

Does your stomach hurt?

Is your head spinning?

Are you warm?

Do you feel pain somewhere?

1. Place your hand where the tension lies, where you can identify your emotion.

Give yourself 10 minutes to experience steps 1, 2 and 3. Take all the time you need to go inside yourself and feel these uncomfortable things. You have to feel in order to heal. Do this with compassion and love for yourself.

Step 4: I welcome

Repeat the following sentence in your head. Adapt the words to your situation and to what resonates the most with you:

"Yes, I am angry/frustrated/sad/afraid... Yes, I'm not ok. It's perfectly normal that I feel like this after what happened. But I'm here for myself. I welcome all that is happening inside me."

Take three deep breaths by breathing in through the nose and out through the mouth.

Step 5: I honour

Finish by thanking the emotion for showing up:

"Thank you, emotion, for opening the door to myself. Thank you for allowing me to heal. Thank you for freeing from the weight of the past."

Tool 1.3: Writing

Writing allows us to note down everything that happens in our mind. The time to write what we feel allows other thoughts to emerge and that help us to go, gradually and increasingly, deeper inside ourselves.

This tool brings feelings and thoughts to reality, as they are written down. It also allows us to let go of what we feel, without complexes or judgment, with all the compassion that we need when we find ourselves invaded by an uncomfortable emotion.

Step 1: Preparing myself

You don't need much to write what you feel. A pen, a page, a calm space. With or without music, it all depends on your preference.

Sit at a table, on a sofa, on your bed. Choose a space where you feel good and where you can let yourself go. Close your eyes. Breath deeply and let rise what comes.

Step 2: I write

Give room to the inner voice that wants to yell, scream, escape, cry, or panic. This voice can express itself here and now. Take the time that is needed to write until relief appears.

What am I feeling?
Why am I sad/angry/frustrated/cross/disappointed/...?
What am I afraid of?
Why does it hurt?
What would I say if I could express myself?

Step 3: I honour

Once you have nothing left to write, once the emotion has passed through you and you feel relieved, write this phrase at the bottom of your page:

"Thank you, emotion, for opening my own door. Thank you for allowing me to heal. Thank you for freeing me from the weight of the past."

Step 4: I burn what I just wrote (optional)

If you wish to do so and if you just used a simple paper, you can burn it. Go outside, preferably in open air, with a stainless steel bowl, matches and your paper. Tear it into several small pieces, place them in the bowl, then burn the corner of one paper to set fire to your unpleasant emotions. Watch the smoke rise and the paper consume itself. Visualize your thoughts flying away and disappearing to alleviate you. These dark ideas will leave you to give to more lightness, calm and trust. It's really satisfying and powerful.

Complementary tool: Grounding

Grounding is a complementary tool that will help you manage your emotions. It complements the three preceding tools without replacing them. You can devote yourself to your grounding whenever you want, without being in the process the Self-Healing Spiral.

What does "being grounded" mean? Imagine a boat without an anchor. There is little chance that it will stay still in the same space. The current, the wind, and the passing of other boats will gradually make it drift. It'll go in one direction, and then another, letting itself get carried by the good will of all that surrounds it. However, if its anchor is pressed well into the sand, it will just move lightly with the wind, it'll turn around the same spot, but never drift.

This image already makes you understand that it is important to be grounded to face life events, little or large storms. Being grounded is to be connected to yourself, listening to your needs. It is being in the present moment, in a conscious way. It's happened to all of us, to quickly put our things away and then not remember where we had put our wallet down, our car keys or another mundane object. This type of simple gesture becomes a reflex, but shows us that we are not always conscious of our actions. We don't really think about the thing that we're doing, but think more about the grocery list, the appointment for the next day, the mail we need to reply to, the bills to be paid, a conversation that upset us, etc. Little by little, our thoughts concerning the past or future accumulate and unground us. Our boat drifts from its center. The more you bring yourself to the present moment, the more grounded you will be. The more grounded you are, the more centered you are. The more centered, the more emotions will pass through you without controlling or drifting you.

From a spiritual point of view, being ground is fully accepting your incarnation. We often use the phrase "having both feet in the ground" to talk about someone being realistic and therefore well-grounded in reality. When we have the head in the clouds, when we dream, when our projects don't come to life, when we often change our mind or have the blues - we are not grounded. We haven't yet accepted to live this human experience fully and wish to return to where we came from. A part of us has chosen incarnation, but this choice is not yet fully accepted and this expresses itself through distraction, a lack of joy, a lack of energy, or projects in the wind.

Thus, being grounded is to transform projects into actions. It is coming down from the stars onto the earth, from the head to the feet, from the idea to its creation. We live in matter and must act with it, even if it is easier to stay in the height of our thoughts.

Being grounded is also to have clear ideas and show lucidity. We learn to take a step back, perceive things in the entirety and not to let ourselves be submerged by a ton of details that distance us from the essentials.

Being grounded is seeing life on the good side, as this grounding brings us joy and energy. We have a positive approach to things while taking the negative aspects into consideration. Like the boat's anchor that prevents it from drifting, your lucidity will allow you to face the water's movements with full trust.

You now understand the importance of grounding. Here are practical tools that will help you stay grounded, your two feet on the ground, but your head surrounded by stars:

- Breathe deeply with the stomach, with ease and relaxation. In your lower stomach, visualize a bowl filling itself with each inhale.
- Walk with bare feet in the grass, when the weather permits it.
- Take hot baths with Himalayan or Epsom salt.
- Think about what you're doing, bring your thoughts to what you are doing instead of the things you'll need to do later.
- Realize small projects having easily attainable objectives, to discover the power you have in your life

- Offer yourself energy healing treatments that will bring you confidence and serenity (Reiki, SAIME, etc.)
- Practice a physical activity that includes an energetic approach (yoga, Tai Chi, Qi Gong etc.)
- From time to time, eat spicy foods to stimulate your body.
- Inhale deeply while visualizing a red light lifting up to the top of the hip then exhale calmly and imagine this light going back down and creating long roots from your feet into the Earth. With each exhale, these roots strengthen and go further down.
- Imagine you are wearing golden hooves. These hooves are heavy. They attach you to the ground and make you go within.[1]

What we learned in this chapter:

- Welcoming and honouring your emotions brings an almost instantaneous relief. It liberates the body and the heart from a weight of the past.
- Welcoming your emotions means that you have to let everything pass through you. Simply embracing them.
- Honouring your emotions means unrolling the red carpet for them and thanking them for the message and healing they bring.
- The above tools also develop emotional intelligence which favors our human relationships.

5

STEP 4 : TRANSMUTE

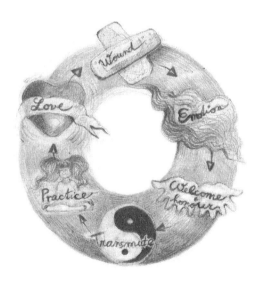

W hen I moved to Montreal to study energy healing, SAIME (Système d'Aide et d'Intervention à la Médecine Énergétique; Help and Intervention System for Energetic Medicine), I had trouble living in a situation where I was uprooted and lonely. Everything was new around me, from the streets to the supermarket shelves, not to mention their different French accent. My senses were constantly stimulated to help me find my way around this new world. The first few weeks were difficult, even though I knew that stepping out of our comfort zone pushes our limits and opens new doors within us. I had actually moved to get out of my cocoon. I therefore accepted this drastic change, synonymous with discomfort, as best I could.

Beyond the studies and the novelty I was looking for, I had also made this choice to find time for myself, far from all the Belgian solicitations. The tourist status preventing me from working, and the sale of the apartment I shared with my ex-husband allowing me to live a few months without a salary, I had decided to devote myself entirely to myself, my passions and my dreams: trips, guitar lessons, yoga, reading books on personal development or spirituality, etc. SAIME private lessons were held only one weekend per month. It gave me all the time and availability I wanted. I had longed for this freedom for a long time. Yet once it was served to me on a silver platter, it made me anxious. I felt like I was doing nothing. I felt like I was filling my days with activities to pass the time. I was not enjoying any of it. I felt nervous on the inside. I felt like I was trying to fill a void, but couldn't really do it. I was in the action while forgetting to *be* before I went into action.

At that time, I was beginning to learn to welcome my emotions. I gave them room when I got inside myself. I let them pass through me and dared to live them, but I felt that it was not enough for me. Aware of the power of our thinking, I wrote several sentences that would do me good, until I came across the one that resonated with me the most. I sat on the edge of the chair and repeated out loud: "Today, I, Eléonore, am worth to give myself time off". I repeated this sentence for several minutes. Very quickly, an emotion rose and tears flowed. That's exactly what it was. Something inside me, my ego and its beliefs, prevented me from enjoying the present moment, because I felt I didn't deserve it. Indeed, I felt like I was wasting my time if I wasn't working. I thought I only had the right to enjoy my freedom and time once my day at work had passed. As the saying which I used to follow to the letter goes, "After the effort, the comfort". If there was no effort, I was not entitled to comfort. At least, that's what I had recorded inside myself. This exercise shed light on these unconscious thoughts.

I repeated my sentence every morning for 21 days, the time it takes for cellular reprogramming to allow for a change in habits. As the weeks went by, I regained pleasure and joy. I was enjoying spending more and more time with myself. I finally dared to devote myself entirely and without any guilt to my passions. The various transmutations I carried out in the weeks that followed, raised several of my blockages and allowed me to find what I had come to seek: healing and reconstruction.

« I am a human being and not a human *doing*. »

This episode also opened my eyes to the way I work. I

realized that I was becoming a *human doing* and not a *human being*. When we are too much into action, we no longer are, we do. We no longer feel, we do. We no longer choose, we do it out of habit. We no longer move forward, we are doing as usual. We no longer live, we survive. We repel the emotions that visit us and throw ourselves even further into the action to forget that there is a visitor in front of the door. We forget that we can simply be, and sometimes we do not even allow ourselves to be.

However, I believe we must learn to *be* again before we *do*. As psychologist Michèle Glorieux taught me: we are what we feel and not what we do. We must learn to feel before anything else. We must get rid of the permanent action to give way to everything that is happening within us. We must get rid of the action, to enter into relaxation and self-hearing. Once we have listened to our feelings, we experience something completely different and our choices change. Our new way of being gives a whole new meaning to our way of *doing* things. Our new way of being makes us want to do other things. Our new way of being places our feelings as a guide in our lives. We no longer survive, we live and feel. We are and that is more than enough.

That was the most important lesson of my first months in exile. Then, it is by allowing myself to be and by observing myself on a daily basis that the Self-Healing Spiral came to me. When we allow ourselves to be, our *doing* takes on a whole new meaning.

Our thoughts create our reality

.   .   .

Following the event that triggered our wound, we have unpleasant emotions and dark thoughts. We criticize ourselves, we devalue ourselves, we feel guilty, we are disappointed by our own attitude and this sequence of thoughts projects us directly into a negative reality. As we saw in the previous chapter, the first thing to do is to welcome and honour what is happening within us. We can talk to the concerned person, talk to our inner child or write down how we feel. We have just gone through three stages that make things uncomfortable: The Wound, The Emotion, Welcoming and Honouring. We are now tilting the balance to the other side with pleasant emotions. We will transform our dark ideas into bright ideas and replace negative thoughts with positive ones. Now comes the stage of Transmutation which reprograms our subconscious, where our fears and limiting beliefs are located.

We have more than 60,000 thoughts a day. It is a huge amount of ideas, negative thoughts, self-criticism, compliments, questions, assumptions, fears, worries, etc. Dr. Joe Dispensa explains[1] that thoughts related to past events will recreate emotions related to the past. These emotions create actions that gradually become habits, routines, beliefs. The body that acts in the present lives in the past, however, because it has habits that have been formed as a result of past events.

In addition, our brains want to help us in the performance of our tasks and support our points of view. In everyday life, the Thalamus helps us select elements that are important to us and showing us that we are right. It believes that we are always making the right choices and wants to help us make those choices even faster. Its objective is to make our lives easier! Gradually, we fall into a vicious circle where we always see life the same way, we do things the same way and express the same emotions, points of view and beliefs.

The only way to change is to get out of our comfort zone by reprogramming our thoughts and making new choices. By thinking differently, we will act differently. It's uncomfortable at first, because the body is in an unknown space, which it doesn't like at all. It feels in danger. But little by little, the comfort zone expands and our new actions, provoked by new thoughts, will offer us a new life. To reprogram our daily lives with emotions, we can use the Transmutation.

Placebo, Nocebo and Lessebo effect

Thoughts have unlimited power and the majority of them come back in a loop without us really being aware of it. They greatly affect our choices and our lives. You know the Placebo effect, don't you? The placebo effect allows a disease to be cured through the power of thought. We will give a child a candy and tell him that it is the only medicine that will make him feel better. In a few hours, he will feel he has recovered "thanks" to what he thinks is a drug, but in reality it is the power of his thinking. The body is the only thing that can heal itself. If we cut ourselves, we'll heal naturally. If we break our legs, the doctor will replace the bone and put a cast on us, but it is the body that will do what is necessary to allow us to walk again. Medications relieve symptoms or speed up the healing process, but the body is the one that really heals itself. Thinking can trigger this healing process.

Robert G. Smith, founder of FasterEFT, has shared some

exciting studies about the power of thought. Doctors divided people into two groups. The first group received treatment with radiation and the second group received false radiation. One third of the second group lost their hair. The power of their thinking caused hair loss when there was no radiation. This is called the Nocebo effect. It is the ability of the mind to produce symptoms when there is no physical cause.

This may seem absurd to you, but I was able to see this Nocebo effect first hand. A few years ago, I was diagnosed with an ovarian cyst. Nothing serious, it was a benign cyst. This happens to more than 20% of women at least once in their lives. The gynaecologist prescribed me a hormonal contraceptive method because it helps to remove the cysts. He suggested me to come back two months later to see how things were going. I had some pain and pinching in my lower abdomen, but the cyst was no more disturbing than that. As the weeks went by, I almost didn't feel it until the pinches reappeared and became more and more powerful. The pain bothered me during simple movements such as walking. I was getting more and more worried because I didn't want an operation and I hoped it wouldn't be necessary. As the day of the appointment approached, the more worried I became, the more uncomfortable the pain became. The day of the appointment, I was paralyzed by fear. This cyst was all I could think of. I couldn't make decisions concerning the following weeks because I was so afraid of surgery. As soon as I arrived at the gynaecologist's office, I told him that I had a bad feeling, because the pain had increased. He calmly examined me and said, "Miss, you have nothing. The cyst is gone, it has melted as it usually does". "Are you sure about this? Really sure?" I replied. "Oh yes, look, there's nothing left. I can even write it down and sign it for you if you want!". I felt deeply ridiculous with my imaginary pain. I had created a film on my own. My thoughts had created pain that evaporated within an hour of that appointment. Wow! I was impressed by the power of my thinking and the impact it had on my body. I had just experienced the Nocebo effect.

In the unlimited powers of thought, there is still a third effect called the Lessebo effect. It occurs when a patient receives real treatment, but is convinced that it will not work. This shows that the expected results are not being achieved. The mind and its thoughts are so strong that they will prevent the treatment from doing what it's supposed to do and block the body's natural healing.

The conclusion presented by Robert G. Smith is that our thoughts in our subconscious mind can create both positive and negative effects, regardless of whether the treatment offered is real or not. Other scientific studies have also shown the impact of the placebo effect and therefore the connection between mind and body. Our subconscious mind decides 95% of our lives, while only 5% of our choices are conscious. Once you know that, it's interesting to go dig into your subconscious and reprogram it, isn't it ?

The brain without denial

Another fundamental information: the brain does not hear negation. If I tell you, "Don't think of a pink elephant", what are you thinking of? A pink elephant, right? So, when you say to yourself, "I'm not going to eat chocolate", your brain records, "I'm going to eat chocolate". In other words, it will make you eat chocolate. It is therefore essential to avoid saying "I don't want this negative thing", but rather "I want this positive thing". This also applies to emotions. Rather than say "I don't want to be sad", say "I want to be confident / well / happy /...".

Sometimes it seems easier to identify what we don't want rather than what we want. This is a question we must ask ourselves every day and the answer can change over time. This step will gradually teach you to express what you want and what you need to balance what you no longer want.

Visualization as reality

In the chapter on emotions, we discovered that a simple thought can create an emotion. Indeed, you only have to think you're missing an important meeting the next day to feel the anxiety rising. Why? Because the brain does not make any difference between what we think and what we really experience. This works for both negative and positive thoughts. Indeed, a 1995[2] study shows us that the imagination of an experience and the experience itself activate the same neurons and stimulate the same areas of the brain.

Let's experience this together: Imagine yourself on a heavenly beach on a Caribbean island. You are surrounded by palm trees, the sea is turquoise, the sand is soft and fine. The sun warms your skin, a light breeze provides the ideal temperature for this well-deserved holiday. You are lying on a deckchair and enjoying this relaxing moment to the fullest. A waiter brings you a delicious refreshing drink. You hold the glass to your lips and enjoy this elixir with coconut, pineapple and banana flavours. You smile and let yourself be rocked by the lapping waves.

So how do you feel when you visualize this situation? Are you relaxed? Maybe you're a little hot because of the sun? Have you tasted the refreshing drink in your mouth or heard the sound of the waves? Indeed, you have just noticed that the brain perceives a visualization as a real event. Our body reacts to it in the same way as well. This applies to both positive and negative thoughts. The transmutation takes advantage of this brain function and pushes us to visualize a bright future. The more we see this same future, the more the brain, thinking that it is reality, will find elements of our everyday life to make us feel the same way. Remember that this is the mission of our Thalamus. It wants to make our lives easier by helping us to reach the same conclusions more quickly.

Change of nature, not setting

Step four is called *Transmutation*, because to transmute means "Transforming something by changing its nature". We will change the nature of our thoughts from negative to positive. We will create a bridge between the conscious and the subconscious to reprogram our subconscious and get out of our "comfort" zone which is not so comfortable after all. This will allow us to overcome our fears, erase our limiting beliefs and get rid of blocks.

This step is based on different concepts, scientifically proven and explained through the previous pages:

- Our thoughts create our reality. What we focus

on, will grow and be realized in one way or
another, as explained by the placebo, nocebo or
lessebo effects.

- The brain does not hear negation.
- The brain does not distinguish between what we
  imagine and what we really experience.
- The brain thinks we are always making the right
  choices and will help us make those same
  choices faster and faster. It will identify in our
  lives the evidence that we are right and that we
  are making the right choices.

Given our habit of thinking the same things over a long
period of time (weeks, months, years), this transmutation
exercise can be difficult to do at first. Indeed, we will thwart
our usual thoughts and reprogram them into something
fairer and more positive. Our ego will not appreciate it,
because it created these emotions and beliefs. It was forced
to do so at some point for our own survival and will feel
threatened if you push it in the opposite direction. You
might hear it protest! A friend, who applied the Self-Healing
Spiral method, told me that when she repeated the
sentence: "*I love myself and I accept myself fully and totally as I
am*", she also heard a second voice early on retorting: "*but no,
you can't love yourself as you are because you can't do this*". The
ego responds and is not ready for change. It does not let us
do the exercise calmly, confuses our thoughts, prevents us
from retaining the sentence, draws our attention to something else... Be reassured, it is completely normal. And that
means above all that you are exactly at the right place.
Persevere and show consistency.

If it's easy for you to do this exercise right from the start.
Great ! It means your little guardian feels safe with you. It is

then more open to change. You will see that the more you do this exercise, the easier it will be and the more it will bring you almost instant relief.

> « Replacing unpleasant emotions with pleasant ones is
> the foundation of our health, life and longevity. »
> Don Tolman[3].

Tool 2: Transmutation

Step 1: I prepare myself

1. Take a pen, a piece of paper and sit in a quiet place where you will not be disturbed. You can play soft music if it helps you to get deeper inside yourself.

2. Take a deep breath.

3. Write or repeat the following sentence:

   « Thank you emotion for being here today. I now choose

to enter a space of peace and tranquility by
transforming the nature of my emotion. »

You can repeat this sentence several times if it feels good.
Observe the changing sensations in your body and see the
openness that is created in you. This sentence aims to tame
your ego so that its resistance is weaker. You are ready to
start.

Step 2: Create the transmutation

Take a moment to look at yourself honestly and kindly.
What are the thoughts that inhabit you? What emotion is
going through you? What situation is problematic? What
did you just welcome in step 3? What's going on inside you?
Give yourself several minutes to understand the situation.
Otherwise, here are some common examples:

I am not good enough... (nice, smart, pretty, funny
enough...)

I don't deserve to... (do myself good, give myself time, be
seen...)

I can't trust you

I don't know if I can do this

I always have to do everything by myself

I am not ready

I don't allow myself to

I don't feel like I belong

I'm afraid to miss out

I'm afraid to commit myself to

I am afraid to be alone

Then transform this negative thought into positive thinking
using the structure below:

« Today, I, (your first name),... »

You can write several sentences that transform this negative thought into positive ones. Look at the one that resonates with you the most and seems to be the most accurate. Find the sentence that does you the most good when you say it out loud or the one that creates the most resistance. Here are some examples:

I am not good enough: Today, I, Éléonore, love myself and accept myself fully and deeply as I am.

I don't deserve to... (do myself good, give myself time, be seen...): Today, I, Éléonore, am worth... Taking care of myself / taking time / being seen and I do it with pleasure.

I can't trust you: Today, I, Éléonore, let go and open myself up to others by trusting them.

I always have to do everything by myself: Today, I, Éléonore, am not alone and dare to ask for the help I need.

I am not ready: Today, I, Éléonore, have all the resources in me to deal with this situation and I know that everything will be fine.

I don't feel like I belong: Today, I, Éléonore, deserve to take my place in my life and in my body and I take it back.

I'm afraid I'm going to lose: Today, I, Éléonore, give myself the right to make mistakes and grow through everything.

I'm afraid to get involved: Today, I, Éléonore, give myself the time I need and I trust that everything will come at the right time.

I'm afraid of...: Today, I, Éléonore, let go and trust that everything happens to me for my own good and personal development.

I am afraid to be alone: Today, I, Éléonore, am rediscovering the pleasure of being alone. I am safe with myself, because I am there for me.

If you can't create a transmutation phrase the first time, don't worry. It takes a little practice. Give yourself time. You can always use the sentence below, because it will cover your wounds with love. This sentence can therefore be used at any time.

« Today, I, Éléonore, love and accept myself fully and deeply as I am. »

Step 3: Transmute

1. Place your dominant hand (right if you are right-handed and vice versa) on the back of your head, where your reptilian brain is located, the cradle of emotions. Place the other hand on your forehead, where limiting beliefs are created.
2. Repeat your sentence aloud for two minutes. Take the time to weigh each word.
3. Remove your hands and continue to repeat your sentence in your head for 3 to 5 minutes. Visualize the positive state you experience with this sentence. You see yourself, surrounded by your loved ones, their attention and affection, as you feel the emotions you pronounce in your head.

If you struggle with this exercice or want me to guide you through it, check out my YouTube video "How to rewire your brain?". You'll find it on my channel *Eléonore de Posson*.

Application

Do this exercise with the same sentence for 21 days in a row. This time is necessary for the renewal of our cells and the integration of new habits. If you forget to do the exercise for a day, you will have to start the cycle again from the beginning. So, apply yourself from the beginning and in three weeks it will all be over!

During this period, you can do the transmutation directly, without having to welcome the emotion first. Indeed, the welcoming of the emotion was necessary at the beginning to target your need and create the appropriate transmutation. Now that you have written and performed it for the first time, you can do this transmutation exercise every morning, for 3 weeks, to better start your day. On the other hand, if this same emotion returns, above all welcome it and then continue in the Self-Healing Spiral with the Transmutation. You will continue your 21-day cycle simply where you are, without having to start all over again on day 1.

This transmutation may seem difficult at first, but it is a real tool for change in the long term. So persevere and be patient if you encounter difficulties in its realization. The more you engage in listening, giving yourself compassion and love, the easier this exercise will be and the healing within your reach.

For other situations that will arise in the future, the ideal is to apply the transmutation stage immediately after the welcoming stage. At that moment, we are at the heart of the emotion and the wound. It is therefore the right time to create the sentence that resonates most with you and then transform the nature of your initial emotion.

What we learned in this chapter:

- Our thoughts create our reality
- Only the body has the ability to truly heal itself
- It is important to transform negative thoughts into positive ones in order to reprogram the subconscious mind
- The Thalamus identifies elements of everyday life that confirm that we are right and encourages us to do the same thing over and over again and to think the same way.
- The brain does not record the negative and focuses on what will be affirmed, without the negative
- Positive thoughts are the foundation of good physical, emotional and mental health
- Check out my youtube video "How to rewire the brain?" if you want to be guided for the transmutation.

6

STEP 5 : PRACTICE

The first few months I spent in Montreal were an exploration of myself. I took the time to rebuild my life in a new way by considering what suited me and no longer suited me. What I wanted and no longer wanted. What still affected me and what I had already healed. These observations gave me the feeling that I could rebuild myself from scratch. I wanted to make the most of it by trying a lot of tools. Observing what was working for me and what wasn't. Every morning, during 21 days, I would recite my transmutation. The need to plan everything and the feeling of not being able to enjoy my time came back a few times. When it surfaced, I would welcome it. I would allow myself to feel the discomfort, the fears, and would release it all on paper. Sometimes I would cry as well. Then I would continue with the transmutation.

That's when I realized that even though the emotion had been treated at the level of the heart and mind, my body was still tense. I felt a tension related to the emotion. Naturally, I sat down crossed legged and started moving to let go of that tension. After fifteen, twenty minutes, all the tension was gone. I felt much better in my body and in my head. I was going back to feeling calm and serene.

Relaxation to physically release our emotions

Step 5 "Practice" is the last active step of our Self-Healing Circle. After welcoming, honouring and transmuting the emotion that has arisen, the body keeps traces of the emotion and it is completely normal. The body is tense, because the emotion stimulates our sympathetic nervous system, which is responsible for stress and activates our muscles. When an emotion passes through us, its objective is to set us in motion, remember its Latin etymological root *emovere* (cf. chapter 3). Our body sends signals to our muscles so that they are ready to react in a second. Our muscles are under tension, in the *fight-or-flight* mode. This mechanism is completely natural and can also be observed in animals. Once the danger is eliminated, animals shake. They shake themselves hard to relieve the tension from their muscles. Have you ever felt relieved by slamming a door right after a fight? It's exactly the same. Babies also have their own tactics to relieve stress and emotions: they cry at the end of the day. The famous crying from 5 to 7 is their way of shaking off the emotions accumulated over the hours. We support these babies, except that we, adults, have forgotten the importance of this antistress.

I'm not telling you to slam doors as soon as something bothers you. Instead I would suggest to consciously bring relaxation back into your body and thus into your mind. Because if the body is calm, the mind calms down immediately. To do this, we will balance the stimulation of the sympathetic and parasympathetic nervous systems. These operate in an alternative way. We use either one or the other. The sympathetic nervous system puts the body into action. It is activated when we play sports, are under stress or under any form of pressure. It is mainly active during the day and will accelerate heart rate, respiratory activity, sweating, etc. This nervous system is associated with adrenaline and norepinephrine. The parasympathetic nervous system puts us at rest. It balances the previous one by allowing the body and its cells to regenerate. It is mainly active at night and causes a general slowing down of the organs in order to make the necessary "repairs". However, in our ultra-active lives, our sympathetic nervous system is over-stimulated during the course of the day. The body needs more time to evacuate the stress accumulated over the day. As part of the Self-Healing Spiral, we will offer this time consciously and voluntarily to our body to relieve emotional stress. In this way, we will eliminate emotions.

Moreover, the time we devote to ourselves is a sacred moment. It improves our relationship with ourselves and gradually increases self-love. Love being the only thing that deeply heals us, this step will bring us even closer to healing.

Therefore, Step 5 "Practice" has a double objective:

- To evacuate the muscular tension created by the emotion. It will bring the body back into a peaceful space, meaning it will activate the parasympathetic nervous system.
- Increase the love and attention we give ourselves.

This chapter will provide you with 4 tools meeting these two objectives. You will be able to choose the ones you are most comfortable with. You will also be able to choose when to implement them. Either in the continuity of step 3 and 4, just after an event has caused an unpleasant emotion to arise. That is, later on the day of the event. Or not directly related to an event, but simply to do you good. This is entirely possible thanks to its dual objective. Indeed, when you take care of yourself, you feel good. This also has a direct impact on the last stage of the Self-Healing Circle: "Love".

.   .   .

We are pure energy

If animals shake, humans have their own way of activating their parasympathetic nervous system. As we explored in the chapter on emotions, we are only energy, pure energy. We even have four sources of energy: physical, emotional, spiritual and mental. The American bestseller by Jim Loehr and Tony Swartz, *The power of full engagement*[1], explains how to juggle with them to be effective, that is, the best version of ourselves. To activate our parasympathetic nervous system, we will use these 4 sources of energy.

Our physical energy is what we generally mean by the word "energy". If we are tired, we have little energy. Taking care of it is as simple as giving time and importance to your body in three ways: eating healthy, sleeping and being physically active. So it's the amount of energy we have.

Our emotional energy is the set of our emotions. They animate us from the intrauterine life where we feel all that our mother feels. Emotional energy is directly related to our performance. In fact, comfortable emotions increase our performance and uncomfortable emotions have a negative impact on it. The more pleasant and comfortable emotions we feel on a regular basis, the more emotional energy we will have and the more effective we will be. This is about the quality of the energy at our disposal.

Our mental energy is composed of our thoughts, our intellect and mainly our ability to concentrate. It is about how we see, understand and interpret things. Mental energy is our ability to be focused as long as we want, on what we want, when we want. It is what allows us to move forward and be effective.

Our spiritual energy connects us to the meaning we give

to our lives. It is our greatest source of motivation. To ensure that we understand each other, I would like to suggest Loehr & Swartz's definition of spirituality, which is not related to religion, but is: "The profound connection to a set of values and a purpose that goes beyond our personal interest". Spirituality can also be defined as "a natural experience that allows the being to flourish in his true greatness. It consists in recognizing the existence of our true self and learning to let ourselves be guided by it". From then on, our spiritual energy will give us the desire and motivation to carry out certain tasks that go beyond our own interest. When our work brings us joy, brings together our passions and allows us to share our gifts, we no longer feel like we are working and no longer count the time that passes, because our motivation is infinite. We have an endless energy! It is the motivation from our spiritual energy that will make the quantity, quality and efficiency of our energy infinite.

These four energies are in correlation with each other. They influence and complement each other. The four tools I present below; Yoga, Meditation, Breath work and Energy healing offer the development of our four energy sources at once. They each meet the dual objective of this step 5 "Practice", which is the release of muscle tension and the increase of self-love. We can use them on two different occasions: after the transmutation when you are applying the Self-Healing Spiral and at any time of the day to take care of ourselves.

In addition, doing these exercises on a regular basis will also increase our vibratory rate, which is, the speed at which energy flows through us. Maintaining a high vibratory rate optimizes our energy, but also protects our personal balance, supports our physical and mental health and makes us feel more joyful. I would advice to start with the tools you are most familiar with and to integrate them into your life on a regular basis in order to get the most out of them. Step 5 is called "Practice" because it suggests a regular, daily, practice.

A healthy mind in a healthy body

Our physical energy is impacting our body and has many functions. It makes us breathe, sleep, digest, reflect and act thanks to an unconscious intelligence within each of us. The body is brilliant. Its nature is to regenerate, but we must allow it to do so by giving it periods of sleep, a balanced diet and physical activity. These three elements are key to maintaining high physical energy.

Sleeping is one of the body's essential needs. Sleep allows the body to regenerate. If we sleep 8 hours a night, 20% of this sleep will be devoted to the regeneration of the body. Each person being different, it is first of all necessary to listen to ourselves, rather than to follow statistics, but this stop time is essential to recharge our batteries. Daytime rest periods, such as a nap or a break from work after 2 intense hours, are also part of good physical hygiene. It is the oscillation between intense activity and rest that will allow the body to move forward until the end of the day without any apparent sign of fatigue. If you find yourself yawning in the middle of the afternoon, why not give your body a 20-minute break by going for a walk, lying on a couch or doing a little meditation? If our bodies send us messages, let's listen to them. They are not happening for no reason.

A healthy, varied and balanced diet is also essential to provide our body with everything it needs. Each body is different and some types of food are suitable for some people and not for others. Food is also influenced by our deep convictions and ecological choices. Countless books each offer their own version of a balanced diet, so I will not devote more than a few lines to this subject. The only advice I could afford to give after having experienced eating disorders would be to eat with conscience, relaxation, while being attentive to our body. What do I want? Am I really hungry? Am I still hungry? Is something bothering me? Have pleasure in feeding your body with good things. Be kind to him, because he takes care of you every day. If eating is a daily challenge for you, learn to establish good eating habits in your life by taking cooking classes or going to a nutritionist. If this has already been done, check your emotions. My personal journey made me realize that our relationship to food is a reflection of our relationship to ourself. Either we eat too much to stifle emotions and push them far inside, or we control absolutely every calorie we swallow, because we are having trust issues and need to control everything. Food is what we use to put to sleep what is bubbling inside us. Food disconnects us from what is happening within us and makes us feel safe. Unfortunately, it only lasts for as long as it takes to swallow the food... We're at peace with our plate when we're at peace with ourself.

Movement is the third foundation of optimized physical energy. From a purely physical point of view, sports strengthen muscles, stretch ligaments, lower cholesterol, maintain the heart, improve blood circulation... The list of physical benefits resulting from regular sports practice is long. Whether it's walking, swimming, team sports or dance classes, find the sport that entertains you and that you will have fun practicing 2 to 3 times a week to take care of your physical energy without stress. And take the work out of the work out ! Make it fun, outdoorsy and entertaining.

Western society attaches great importance to Physical energy. However, it is just as important as the other 3; emotional, mental and spiritual. If you want to kill four birds with one stone and take complete care of yourself, the next tools will become your best allies.

Yoga, a complete practice

Yoga, Tai Chi or Qi Gong are ancient practices coming straight from Asia. Their movements support our physical development, but also stimulate our energy structure, which supports and develops our emotional, mental and spiritual energy. If you already practice one of these three disciplines, you will have noticed that one hour of yoga is more than just one hour of sport. You finish feeling deeply relaxed, more connected to yourself and have a deep sense of lightness. As a yoga teacher, it was obvious to me to share about this practice, because it changed the relationship I had with myself, my body and others.

Yoga is now very popular and mainstream. More than just a fashion, it attracts a lot of new followers every year, as it has a proven track record in stress management, anxiety, depression, insomnia and eating disorders. In an interview with Live Science[2] magazine, Dr. Loren Fishman, an American doctor and yoga teacher, tells us that "it thickens the layers of the cerebral cortex, the part of the brain associated with studying, and increases neuroplasticity, allowing us to learn new things and change the way we do things".

Stephen Cope is a therapist and director of the Institute

for Extraordinary Living in Massachusetts. He leads a program called "Yoga and the Brain" in which studies are conducted that analyze the effect of Yoga on the brain through MRIs and other advanced techniques. Stephen Cope explains that Yoga reduces the amount of cortisol in the body. Excess cortisol, the main stress hormone, can cause many physical disorders such as decreased immunity, hypertension, insomnia, obesity, loss of memory, etc. Its decrease is therefore always welcome! These studies also show that Yoga releases the trio of hormones of happiness, namely serotonin, dopamine and GABA[3]. These three neurotransmitters bring a feeling of satisfaction and deep relaxation. They are usually prescribed as medications for people suffering from anxiety or depression. One hour of Yoga therefore directly affects our level of anxiety.

But it doesn't stop there: the neurologist and former yoga teacher at the Yoga Society of New York, Sarah Dolgonos, explains that it stimulates the parasympathetic nervous system that restores the nervous balance. When it is activated, "the blood is directly directed to our endocrine glands, digestive organs and lymphatic circulation. It reduces the cardioid rhythm and blood pressure", she tells. Our body then enters a state of regeneration and natural healing. It eliminates stored emotions, accumulated stress and strengthens our precious nervous system.

Beyond these scientific explanations, it is my personal experience that has taught me that Yoga is much more than a sport. The first time I found myself on a mat, I was 18 years old. Yoga wasn't trendy at all back then. I had intense back pain after an accident and my mother suggested me to join to her Wednesday evening yoga class. Very soon, I couldn't do without it. The classes allowed me to build up my back, but above all they allowed me to have an hour to myself.

During that hour, I would give up everything. I would stop thinking, clear my mind and bring my focus on my breath. Sometimes, at the end of the course, tears would even come up without me understanding why. The gentle movement and some postures release emotions. They stimulate our endocrine glands and relax the nervous system so that our body can release all the tensions it has stored.

« Find your own movement, your own alignment, to create your own life »

Over the years, Yoga became a bigger part of my life. One day I decided I wanted to deepen the teachings I was hearing in class and felt called to teach. I started with a Hatha Yoga Teacher Training in India, then Strala Yoga in New York City. Hatha Yoga is the most traditional Yoga; Strala Yoga probably the most modern. But both share the same point of view: "Sthira Sukham Asanam" which means that the practice must be performed in comfort.

Strala Yoga is influenced by Tai Chi and proposes to create "your own yoga". The idea behind it is simply that we all have different bodies. Man, woman, small, tall, round, thin, each body has a different history of accidents, injuries, events... It is not possible that all these different bodies have the same alignment. Everyone must find their own alignment and rhythm. Rigidity and speed are often part of Western yoga classes that ultimately cause more stress and tension. The idea of performance remains in our minds, even on the mat. However, we are already spending our days under pressure and must offer relaxation windows to our body. Strala Yoga underlines the fact that mouvements should be done without tension. In a gentle, relaxed and unique way, as everyone has its own way of doing things and goes its own pace. Even practiced in a gentle way, it is still an active practice where the shower is welcome afterwards.

During my teacher training, I realized our usual way of moving was absolutely not serving us. Tara Stiles and Michael Taylor, the co-founders of Strala Yoga, changed my way of living. This discovery fundamentally changed the way I play sports, but above all the way I approach everyday life and its challenges. Before, I used to add strength and tension to my sports practices whether I was running, swimming, skiing, tennis... I also used to push myself when facing a personal or intellectual challenge. I had the impression that if I didn't make an effort, I wouldn't get anywhere. I had to sweat, I had to struggle, I had to suffer to "get there". It is a belief that we all have and with which we grow. We will deprive ourselves to lose weight, we will work tirelessly for hours to complete a file, we will impose a rigid and intense structure to reach our objectives. However, a strategy made of ease, pleasure and listening to oneself takes us much further. Strala Yoga teaches that in all simplicity and on a yoga mat. The strategy of *No Pain, No Gain* simply does not work.

Why the No Pain, No Gain strategy does not work ?

In their New York studio, Tara and Mike show us how it is easier to get into a handstand, with ease by using your breath, rather than by forcing yourself and "throwing" yourself upside down. We observe, surprised. We then learn why we are addicted to difficulty, when ease and conscious breathing can take us much further, much more easily, on the mat, but also in life. The *No Pain, No Gain* Strategy is rooted in us for four reasons; chemical, neurological, psychological and cultural[4].

First of all, we are chemically addicted to stress. We are so addicted that when we have the opportunity to relax on vacation, we can no longer do it and we are already projecting ourselves into the stress of the to-do list of the first day back home. From a physiological point of view, our body releases a cocktail of hormones made of adrenaline, dopamine, cortisol and endorphins when we are under stress. Our sympathetic nervous system is activated and our muscles are tightened to help us escape danger. When we were prehistoric men who had to flee to avoid being swallowed by a bear, lion or shark, this stress was necessary to save our skin. But the human body can't handle stress for more than 2 minutes. Yet today, we are subject to it on a permanent basis. Living with this cocktail gives us great sensations and makes us feel alive. We become addicted to it because it brings us pleasure (endorphin and dopamine) and our brain will also detect the elements that allow us to experience this pleasure again. But when consumed to excess, it prevents the parasympathetic nervous system from doing its job of regenerating us. Our performance capacities are limited, our digestive and reproductive organs are dysfunctional and we easily get sick. We have lost the balance between these two nervous systems and quickly fall into the famous burn-out that is on the front page of medical certificates.

The second reason is neurological, that is, it concerns

our habits. Our body attaches great importance to everything we do and deduces that we always make the right choice. He then seeks to help us by making this gesture, attitude or choice easier and simpler by myelinating neural pathways. However, the most appropriate choice is not always made. The more we make this type of choice, the faster and easier it will be, because our brain wants to make it easier for us. Before we even know it, we have bad habits that our brains have found good, because they have deduced that we were always doing the right thing. As Tara Stiles says: "If our body pays so much attention to everything we do, maybe we should too?".

Then comes the psychological reason: "We do what we believe". Our beliefs determine us and it is important to analyze them to see if they limit us in our lives. Let me illustrate this with an example that regularly appears in yoga classes. Strala Yoga promotes ease, relaxation, tension-free movement, yet many people think they need to be flexible to be able to do yoga. So they spend most of the class pulling on their muscles. They push themselves, surpass themselves to achieve the flexibility they think they need so much. Stress and difficulty were the key words of their practice when this same hour of class could have brought relaxation and ease to these students. They think they are following the ease shown by the teacher, but their beliefs push them to surpass themselves. They find themselves in a difficult zone rather than a relaxation zone, without the slightest awareness of it.

Finally, the fourth and last reason that makes us act with stress and difficulty is the cultural reason. As I explained earlier, our society convinces us that hard work is key to achieving this. If we introduced ourselves by saying that harmony and ease were better strategies, our entourage would certainly think we are out of line. Yet, if you have a look at top athletes, they perform while they are in their comfort zone and get surprising results when they approach the challenge with ease. Of course, when you start out, your comfort zone is small and then it gradually expands without strength, difficulty or stress.

To conclude, I will repeat Tara's words: "It is important that we really think that the best way to do this is by feeling good all along the way. Because the way we go where we go is the way we will feel when we get there. It is important to practice this, not just think it or say it. Actually practice it". If you want to feel good when you get there, you have to feel good all along the way. If we are looking for self-love, we must approach this journey with gentleness, kindness and compassion... With love, simply put. If you want to feel proud, happy and fulfilled once the goal is reached, then you just have to feel proud, happy and fulfilled all along the way, facing every obstacle and every difficulty. Little by little, I realized that the path was just as important, if not more important than the objective. Ease and kindness are the key to enjoying the path and its destination. You see that the practice of Yoga goes far beyond physical practice ?

« The way we feel when we reach the goal is a reflection of our path »

Now that we have discovered that we are all addicted to stress and difficulty, you are probably wondering how to unlearn this "reflex". I suggest you follow the advice[5] of Strala Yoga co-founder Michael Taylor, who studied Body-Mind Medicine at Harvard and Alternative Medicine and Psychology at Oxford.

He starts by suggesting that we learn to go slower and simpler. Whether it is a sporting activity or a lifestyle choice, we are generally good at going fast. This slowness and simplicity allow us to observe what we do and what is not necessarily good for us. We can then replace these choices with better movements, whether it is sport; or better emotions, in the case of human relationships. Take the time to go slowly and observe yourself to understand where you are complicating your life for no reason whatsoever.

« Be yourself, all the others are already taken »

Then we have to relearn how to find our own way. We tend to copy others, whether it is the Yoga class or our next vacation destination. Yet we have our own wisdom in us that shows us the way. The more we learn to listen to it, the easier it will be to have a health that supports us in everything we do. Let us dare to play our own roles. We can learn this on a yoga mat and then apply it to our lives so that we can be the best version of ourselves.

« The power of movement is to relieve stress »

Finally, he advises us to learn to move better. "Move better" means moving in all directions, with all parts of your body, in ease and simplicity by doing what is pleasant for us. So it doesn't mean pushing your limits by forcing yourself, blocking your breathing and adding tension to your movements. This difference is the one that allows us to reach a state of consciousness and self-awareness that optimizes our physical, emotional, spiritual and mental energy. This "good" movement is the one that eliminates stress. Slowly realized, it takes us out of the state of continuous tension to which we are addicted to allow the body to regenerate itself and show more performance. It also releases the emotions that remain stuck in us. Gradually, we are accessing a space where good decisions about our food, work and relationships will be easier to make, as we become more aware of what is good for us. It's not just about moving to get there, but it's about moving better. We can learn to apply this on a yoga mat to gradually introduce these new habits into our lives. Let's do things slowly, simply, uniquely and easily to reduce our stress, restore our nervous system, improve our ability to study, eliminate stored emotions and be more at peace with ourselves.

Movement is a wonderful tool in step 5 of the Self-Healing Circle. Yoga takes care of our physical energy by using our whole body. Our emotional energy is improved by reducing stress and anxiety. Our mental energy is stimulated by the concentration required on breathing and our spiritual energy will be amplified by the silence, meditation or general well-being felt at the end of a class. However, if Yoga does not inspire you, find the practice that does. Walking, running, team sports... We are all different, so it is important that you find your practice, your movement.

Don't just do what I advise you to do, do what is good for you and does you good. I insist.

For those of you who are ready to go, here is a 20-minute sequence that you can do as soon as you are in the Self-Healing Circle and want to release an emotion that has just been transmuted in step 4.

Tool 3.1: 20 minutes of gentle Yoga

Start with your legs crossed. Close your eyes. Breathe in through your nose, let the inhale lift you up and exhale through your mouth. Repeat this three times. Sway gently from side to side to better find your center. Then inhale by raising your right arm, exhale and lean to your left side. Stay here a few breaths. Inhale as you raise your right arm to return to your center. Do the same on the other side.

Then, lean forward and bring your face near your crossed legs. Stay there for 10 breaths. Gently climb up by pressing on your hands.

Bring your heels together. Place your hands on your feet and move your knees slightly up and down. Then open your feet outwards with your hands. Gently lean forward and let yourself go down a little more with each exhalation. Stay there for 10 breaths. Then, open the right leg on the side, put your right hand in front of your knee and lean over your leg. Stay there for 5 breaths. Do the same on the other side.

At your own pace, get on all fours in table position. Breathe in by lifting your head and arching your back, exhale, bring your head in and roll your back. Do this 3 times, then raise your hips and stretch your legs to bring your heels to the ground in the position of the downward dog.

Breathe in, lift your right leg, then exhale and place your right foot between your hands. Let your hips down and look forward. Sway gently your body from left to right to open the hip. Tilt the body weight back and bring your hips back above your knees and stretch the front leg. Breathe here.

Then bring the upper body forward and slightly to the left, to release the weight on your right leg and bring it back. Raise your hips and do the same on the left side.

Then, lower your hips on your heels in child pose and enjoy this moment of relaxation for 5 breaths. Bring your arms back to your body and stay for another 5 breaths. Gently lift the upper part of the body. Inhale and lift your arms, exhale and put your right hand on your left knee, look behind you. Stay three breaths. Inhale, raise your arms and do the same on the left. Come back on all fours and raise your hips to go into downward dog.

Raise your right leg, bend your knee and place your knee next to your right hand. Find a comfortable position and lean forward in the pigeon pose. Stay there for 10 breaths and then slowly climb back up. Press on your hands, lift your hips and move up into the inverted triangle to perform the pose on the left side.

Once this is done, bring the right leg forward and place both feet on the floor, knees bent.

Stretch out your arms in front of you, inhale, then exhale by leaning backwards. Go up by inhaling, and down by exhaling. Do this 5 times. Unroll your back to the ground. Pass the right leg over the left knee, then drop the knees to the left and look to the right. Breathe deeply 5 to 10 times. Raise both knees, release the leg and lift your pelvis to position yourself correctly in the centre of the mat. Do the same on the left.

Then bend your knees and grab the bottom of your foot. Push your knees to the ground. After 5 breaths, release your legs and let them fall gently to the floor. Lie in savasana for several minutes, letting the body to integrate the benefits of this practice.

Then, at the end of these relaxing minutes, turn to the side and press down on the floor to get up. Come to a comfortable sitting position with your legs crossed. Namasté.

You will find short, 15minutes, yoga practices on my youtube channel. Search my name on the youtube search bar : Eléonore de Posson + Yoga. And Enjoy !

Meditation

Meditation is the second tool allowing to take care of our 4 sources of energy and making us switch to the parasympathetic nervous system. This practice leads us to close our eyes and focus on one element, whether it is breathing, a part of the body, a candle, a mantra... When we meditate, our breathing fills our body with energy. The relaxation of the body releases tensions and emotions, the concentration stimulates our mental energy and the silences observed between our thoughts puts us in direct contact with our soul, source of the spiritual energy.

In his book *The art of méditation*[1] Matthieu Ricard, a French Buddhist monk, teaches us that "Meditation is a practice allowing to cultivate and develop certain fundamental human qualities, in the same way that other forms of training teach us how to read, play a musical instrument or acquire any other skill. Etymologically, the Sanskrit and Tibetan words, translated into English by "meditation", are respectively *bhavana*, which means "to cultivate" and *gom*, which means "to become familiar". It is mainly a matter of becoming familiar with a clear and fair vision of things and cultivating qualities that we all have within us, but which remain in a latent state as long as we do not make the effort to develop them". The qualities to which Matthieu Ricard refers are selfless love and compassion. Indeed, a study published in 2004 in the PNAS, *Proceedings of the National Academy of Science*, co-authored by Matthieu Ricard, reveals that the brain activity of meditators is very high in areas related to pleasant emotions as well as those related to movement planning and maternal love. The famous Buddhist monk explains this by saying that "Compassion generates total availability to the other: it can therefore be used to act".

On the other side of the globe, the American Sylvia Boorstein, a psychologist and author of five books on meditation and Buddhism, says that: "Meditation does not change life. Life remains fragile and unpredictable. Meditation changes the heart's ability to accept life as it is".[2] Indeed, the greatest gift of meditation is to bring us back to ourselves. In a world overwhelmed by activity and external stimuli, this practice stops us for a moment and teaches just to *be*. Our two experts agree that the practice of meditation offers a clearer and more accurate vision of events happening to us.

From a physical, emotional and mental perspective, we know that meditation has many beneficial effects on our health; improving attention span, developing compassion, strengthening the immune system, but also reducing stress, anxiety, anger and the risk of relapse in people who have been affected by depression. These benefits are apparent as early as 8 weeks if you engage in a regular 30-minute daily practice.

From a more spiritual point of view, meditation can bring a sense of communion. "I had a feeling of energy centered on me, which went towards infinite space and then came back to me with a deep feeling of love. The borders were dissolving. I felt intensely connected to everything", says Buddhist Michael Baime[3]. In 2002, he was examined with a fine-tooth comb in the laboratory of Andrew Newberg and Eugene d'Aquili, two neurophysiologists from the University of Pennsylvania. As shown in the drawing below[4], there's a decrease in blood flow to the upper parietal lobes.

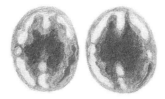

This part of the brain is intended to process information from time and space and distinguishes between self and non-self. "If the sensory influx is prevented from entering this region, as in meditation, then the brain perceives the self as endless, being linked to everything and anything". explains Andrew Newberg[5]. However, the study does not conclude whether this feeling of communion is caused by the decrease in blood flow or whether this decrease is only the consequence of this communion. It is up to each person to choose their answer.

My personal experience made me discover that meditation was a journey from the outer world to the inner world. Often, it put me in contact with an inner wisdom that seemed to advise me. As Roger Gabriel[6] of the Chopra Center, founded by Deepak Chopra, explains, meditation gives room to silence between our thoughts. These follow each other quickly, but are spaced a moment apart from each other. The more we meditate, the longer the silence between our thoughts gets longer. This silence is our soul. This silence is made of infinite possibilities, because our thoughts are infinite. You can compare meditation to a dive in a swimming pool. When you get out, you get wet and covered in drops. These drops are the infinite possibilities that are within us and that we bring back into our daily lives after a meditation. The more we regularly encounter this calm and infinite possibilities, the more we bring these possibilities back into our daily lives.

From a practical point of view, starting meditation can seem both exciting and intimidating. From then on, guided meditations are more and more popular, as they facilitate this new learning. The practitioner is guided by a voice for about ten minutes. They therefore easily become part of a morning routine and usually focus on a particular theme.

Here below, you'll find a meditation I created to increase my self-confidence. I repeated these sentences to myself every morning to rebuild my love for myself and start my days with confidence. For an optimal effect, I advise you to do this meditation for 21 days. If you start meditation, know that like a muscle, it trains and improves over the weeks. Follow the 3 tips [7] from the Chopra Center:

1. Do as little as possible. The less you do, the more results you will get.
2. Thoughts are part of the experience. Accept them and let them go immediately.
3. Don't have any expectations. You meditate for the benefits you will see in your daily life and not for the meditation experience itself.

At the end of this meditation, you will apply the sign of Infinite Love and Gratitude to your heart. This sign, meaning "I love you" in American sign language, is being taught by Dr. Darren Weissman, American author and kinesiologist. The kinesiological muscle test has proven that this sign of Infinite Love and Gratitude positively affects anyone who applies it to themselves[8]. To do this, fold the middle and ring fingers on your palm and open your thumb outward.

Tool 3.2: Guided meditation

Sit comfortably on a chair or on the floor with your legs crossed. Keep your back straight, but relaxed.

Breathe in through the nose in 4 steps. Exhale through your mouth in 7 steps. Do this 3 times. Then, breathe in through your nose only.

Surrender to the present moment.

Let this moment support you.

The present moment asks you nothing, it accepts you exactly as you are.

Feel the ground under you, it supports you.

Release your tensions and doubts.

Repeat the next statements in a low voice or in your head, reminding yourself that you are who you are and that it is fine:

I love myself

I accept myself

I forgive myself

I am proud of myself

I'm here for myself.

I'm enough, much more than enough
I am greatly loved
Everything is fine, everything will be fine

Visualize a person you deeply love. Feel this love and send it back to yourself. Feel all this love circulate throughout your body and all your cells. You radiate with joy, abundance and peace. Place the sign of infinite Love on your heart and bathe in this love.

You can download an MP3 of this meditation on my website : www.eleonoredeposson.com/freetools

Pranayama Breathing

Day and night, we breathe. This is done completely unconsciously. Yet, when we breathe consciously and induce a certain rhythm, we can calm or stimulate our body and mind as we please. The power of breathing is much bigger than we think.

The Sanskrit word Pranayama, derived from the practice of Yoga, consists of two elements: The *Prana*, which is the vital energy within each of us; and the *yama*, which is its extension. Breathing exercises, called *Pranayama*, therefore circulate energy within us. It flows through pranic channels which are energy channels called *Nadis* in India or *Meridians* in China. You can associate them with our nervous and endocrine systems.

The practice of Pranayama has many benefits. Some will aim to stimulate you such as the *Bhastrika* or the *Kapalabhati*. Others will bring you relaxation such as *Ujjayi* or *Nadi Sodhana*. All will benefit you from circulating the Prana and keep energized. Maintaining a good level of this vital energy is essential to be in good physical, emotional, mental and spiritual health. Here is the list of the benefits of Pranayama Breathing:

Physical Energy, Your Body:

- Stabilizes blood pressure
- Increases energy (especially *Bhastrika* and *Kapalabhati*)
- Relaxes muscles and nervous system
- Increases immunity

Emotional Energy, your emotions:

- Reduces stress
- Brings calm and serenity
- Increases the sense of well-being

Mental Energy, your ability to concentrate:

- Strengthens concentration

Spiritual Energy, your mind, the meaning of your life:

- Increases listening to oneself
- Increases intuition
- Increases self-confidence and confidence in life

The exercise I'm about to share with you is the *Anuloma-Viloma*. It is part of the *Nadi Sodhana* family, which in Sanskrit means "purification of the nadi". These breathing exercises are known to calm us down quickly and eliminate any tension in the body and mind. *Anuloma-Viloma* has been one of my favorite tools for a long time. I learned this breathing at the age of 18, when Yoga entered my life. I use it as soon as I feel a really strong emotion showing up. Whether it is stress before an interview, panic or sleeplessness, this breathing exercise has already saved me more than once. *Anuloma-Viloma* is effective in calming down because it balances the two hemispheres of the brain. The right nostril is connected to the left hemisphere, the brain of logic, analysis and rationality. The left nostril is linked to the right hemisphere where emotions, creativity and intuition are housed. When emotions overwhelm us, the right hemisphere is too stimulated, preventing us from using the left hemisphere to think. A rebalancing is necessary to restore harmony in itself. This exercise, magical to me, allows this in less than 10 minutes.

When to use Anuloma-Viloma?

This Pranayama exercise is performed in several cases:

- When you follow the Self-Healing Circle and complete steps 3, 4 and 5 one after the other.
- When you are **in crisis**, overwhelmed by panic or other strong emotions. The rebalancing provided during this exercise will calm you down in a few minutes.
- To relax during the day, to focus before a presentation, before going to sleep, to face stress...

Tool 3.3: Anuloma-Viloma

Step 1: I prepare myself

Sit comfortably in a quiet area where you will not be disturbed.

Bend your right hand as shown in the attached drawing with the index finger and the middle finger lowered into your palm.

Step 2: I Practice

1. Close your eyes. Breathe in and out through both nostrils.

1. Place the thumb on the right nostril. Start the
    first cycle:

Breathe in through the left nostril, 4 seconds.

Close both nostrils and keep your lungs full for 4
seconds.

Exhale through the right nostril, 4 seconds.

Keep your lungs empty for four seconds.

Breathe in through the right nostril, 4 seconds.

Close both nostrils and keep your lungs full for 4
seconds.

Exhale through the left nostril, 4 seconds.

Keep your lungs empty for four seconds.

You have just completed the first cycle. Always end the cycle
by exhaling from the left nostril.

1. Continue as above to achieve 10 cycles.

Energy Healing

I don't want to repeat myself for the tenth time, but we are only pure energy. From then on, it is obvious that another way to take care of yourself is to offer yourself an energy treatment. This gentle and natural approach brings harmony back into the body. Best of all, it will not require any effort on your part.

All energy treatments are different, but from the same source, this invisible world where everything interacts with everything. Among the most famous are Reiki from Japan, the Barbara Brennan school founded in Miami, or the S.A.I.M.E.[1] treatments from Quebec. Amazonian shamans also have their own techniques to cleanse energetic bodies. From the 4 corners of the globe, you will discover different ways of doing it. There are no good or bad ones, they are simply different, stronger or softer. These treatments are not similar to massages, but are carried out by applying hands to specific places on the body or by movements around the body.

Energy healing will restore the balance of energies within us. Dr Sandra Huyghen, Doctor of Life Sciences, MBA graduate, international coach, author and lecturer, has carried out numerous studies on the impact of energy on our bodies. Thanks to electrophotometry, an analysis measuring the photons of light emitted by the body, she carries out very precise[2] personalized assessments, as shown in the drawing below.

In the drawing on the left, we see the state of an energetic structure before an energy healing treatment. It contains energy holes or nodes. The drawing on the right shows the energy structure after a treatment. Balance and harmony are restored. At the end of it, the first result felt is that of our emotional energy. Relaxation, confidence and lightness are the feelings that inhabit anyone getting up from a treatment table. Even if it is not visible to the naked eye, the physical plane will also have benefited greatly from the treatment as you can see above. In the short term, physical pain can be reduced and in the long term it can even be treated. Sleep will also be improved. Mental and spiritual energies will also have been affected but this result will be seen after a few days thanks to the implementation of projects, a better grounding, a greater intuition, more confidence in oneself and in the future...

The Chakras

Energy healing treatments heal our body through our energy structure which is composed of chakras and subtle bodies. Although you may not understand how they work, I would like you to remain open to the fact that they exist. There are many things I don't understand, such as electricity or WiFi; however, this does not prevent me from benefiting from it. Taking care of our energy brings harmony and well-being, such as pressing a switch brings light into a room.

The chakras are found in many ancient medicines such as Indian Ayurvedic Medicine, Traditional Chinese Medicine, Shamanism... These are energy centers, like vortexes, that rotate. Chakra literally means "wheel" in sanskrit. The chakras are like rotating wheels where energy passes through. They are gateways to and from energy. Our experiences, our emotional, mental and spiritual experiences will be imprinted in our chakras, which can unbalance them or weaken their activity. Energy healing will focus on rebalancing the chakras to harmonize our energy. There are 7 major chakras in our spine. In reality, we have a total of 360 chakras which are all related to one of these 7. Each chakra has a function, a vibratory color, a sound and a mantra to which it reacts. Each of them is responsible for a particular aspect: financial independence, sexuality, self-confidence, love, communication, imagination, intuition...

The first chakra is the *Muladhara*, also called root chakra or base chakra. It is located at the base of the spine. This chakra is the meeting place between the Spirit and the matter where the Kundalini rests. Kundalini, symbolized by a snake, is the spiritual energy that rises in the spine after years of meditation practice. It brings an awakening of consciousness that leads to an understanding of the world and the universe. The function of this chakra is to maintain physical awareness and grounding, but also our relationship to money. Its colour is bright red. It allows you to be: "I am".

The second chakra is *Swadisthana* or Hara. It is found at

the level of the genital organs and impacts our sexual development, general well-being and sense of abundance. It is closely related to matter and what we feel. It also represents the place we are taking in the world. If we are aware of our inner power and the choices we must make for our personal evolution, this chakra will work ideally. The first and second chakras are very close to each other and influence each other. Its color is orange. It allows you to feel: "I feel".

The third chakra is the *Manipura* or Solar Plexus. It's in the middle of the belly, below the lungs. It is the centre of all our emotions. It allows us to bring our ideas into action and generally compensates for the excesses of the mind, personality or other minor centres. It holds our confidence and self-esteem. Its color is yellow. It allows you to do: "I do".

The fourth chakra is the *Anahata*, the heart chakra. It is the middle chakra, between the top 3 and bottom 3. It allows the encounter between the energy of the earth and the celestial energy, the fusion of the material and the spiritual symbolized by two triangles that cross and form a star. He takes care of our joy, love and sense of peace. It is the cradle of forgiveness and compassion. This chakra is connected to the two minor chakras found in each palm of the hand with which therapists perform their energy healing. The care therefore comes directly from the heart... Its color is green. It allows us to feel Love and to love: "I love".

The fifth chakra is the *Vishuddha*, the throat chakra. It is the centre of communication, the organ of creative speech, that allows us to express ourselves and share our feelings, thoughts, emotions and ideas. When Man expresses the truth in thought, word and deed, he does so through the center of the throat. Its color is blue. It allows the expression: "I speak".

The sixth chakra is the *Ajna*, or the third eye. It is located between the two eyebrows and allows you to "see" certain things. It is the cradle of our intuition and imagination. It develops through Yoga and meditation. When the third eye is at its peak, we are guided by our intuition, we communicate with the world and can receive messages for our lives. We trust in ourselves and in Life and live in consciousness. Consciousness of the way we look at ourselves and others, awareness of our actions and their consequences, but also awareness of the present moment. Its color is purple. It allows you to see differently, "I see".

The seventh and last chakra is the *Sahasrara*, the crown chakra. It is located on the top of the head and is often represented by a lotus with a thousand leaves. This chakra is the psycho-emotional result of the previous chakras, the more balanced they are, the faster the *Sahasrara* will turn. If the "snake" of *Kundalini* rises to this chakra, then we speak of illumination, *Samadhi*. We enter into unity, this feeling of fusion with everything around us. That's when "I understand". Its colours are white and brown.

Tool 5.4: Treating yourself with energy healing

Giving yourself an energy healing treatment is a wonderful gift. This gentle and natural approach fills your cells and your whole body. The serenity and joy felt at the end of a treatment are profoundly healing. You have to live it to understand it. You can offer yourself a treatment when certain physical or emotional symptoms appear: fatigue, stress, discouragement, uncertainty, pain... Or simply to harmonize your energy balance and make it a preventive medicine. One treatment per month is ideal to maintain harmony in oneself. A professional therapist will provide you with the treatment you need whether it is Reiki, SAIME or coming another school.

Energy balance is important to ensure physical, emotional, mental and spiritual health. It keeps our frequency high, which allows energy to flow properly within us. This helps us enormously on the path to healing and the development of our gifts. You'd never leave your house without brushing your teeth, would you? Oral hygiene is essential. Be aware that energy hygiene is just as important, if not more so.

However, I would like to emphasize here the importance of confiding in a professional. The field of energy has developed considerably in recent years and this is very good for opening our consciences, but it has also brought to light people who abuse our trust. Some ill-intentioned people could waste your time and money. A simple advice I could give you is to make sure that the person you are confiding in is serious. Do they have any diplomas? Who informed you about them? Do they "feel" right? What does your intuition tell you?

Now you have many practical tools to feel better, free yourself from emotional stress and take care of your four energy sources. To begin, select the tool with which you have the most affinity among the four presented above and gradually integrate it into a daily routine. Take it easy and give yourself time. It generally takes 21 consecutive days for a habit to take root. Evolution is better than revolution!

Once you have mastered this tool, replace it with another one, expand your comfort zone and see the difference over time. If these exercises do not appeal to you, other tools by energy type are provided in the appendix. I insist again on letting you choose those with whom you are most comfortable. All our subtle bodies and their energies influence each other so a simple exercise in one category will also impact the rest of your energies. Do all this lightly and with the pleasure of taking care of yourself to improve the effects.

The ultimate goal of all these tools is to bring you wellness and bring you closer to healing. The initiative to take care of yourself regularly as well as the well-being brought to you will have a direct effect on the Love you have for yourself. Love and Self-acceptance are essential in our Self-Healing Circle, because they are the means to heal you and to elevate you in the Spiral of Self-Healing.

What we learned in this chapter:

- Emotion is finally released by relaxing our muscles, through movement, breathing or meditation.
- We are pure energy. We have 4 sources of energy: physical, emotional, mental and spiritual.
- Our energy structure is composed of 7 chakras that should be regularly maintained for good physical, emotional, mental and spiritual health.
- Choose your favorite tool and make it part of your daily routine today. Promise you'll stick to it for 21 days. Feel free to write to me to share your experience!
- Make sure to download all the free tools to support you. You'll find them on www.eleonoredeposson.com/freetools

STEP 6 : LOVE

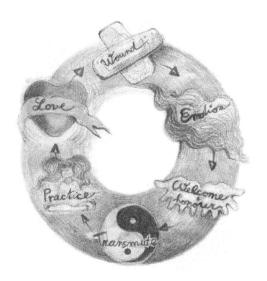

O n a February day, while I was in India for a Hatha Yoga teacher training, I started to imagine myself as a teacher, when I suddenly found myself thinking: "It won't work. I should lose at least five kilos if I want to be credible". Self-criticism, you know what I mean? I was convinced I would not attract students if I kept the same weight when I was neither round nor thin, just normal. Soon, a second small voice came into the conversation: "It is not the weight that determines the quality of a Yoga teacher. It is her passion, her teaching, her commitment, the individual attention she offers to her students and the messages she transmits to open everyone's consciousness". This second, more caring voice made me realize that I was constantly criticizing myself because I did not find myself "enough": not pretty enough, not thin enough, not smart enough, not nice enough, not funny enough, not sociable enough, not disciplined enough, not talented enough, just not good enough. In other words, I didn't love myself. And it is only at the age of 30 that I realized it, thanks to the intervention of this second little voice that I heard in my head in the middle of a Yoga class. But how can we love ourselves? I was then aware of the problem, but I had no idea where to start. I went back to my room after the class, and did the first thing I thought of: I googled "How to love yourself."

Learning to love ourselves

No one teaches us how to love ourselves. My parents could have taught me to love myself. Logically, they could have been the initiators of this path. But how can we ask adults who have never learned to love themselves to teach their children to love themselves? How can we ask this from a generation that thinks that taking care of oneself is selfish? It's as if one caterpillar had to teach another caterpillar to fly: it's an impossible mission. Yet they covered us with tenderness, support and everything they thought was good for us. They always did their best with all the knowledge they had, but my parents didn't teach me to love myself, because they just didn't know they had to do it. I'm not throwing stones at them, on the contrary, they gave me the possibility to discover it myself. Today, they also have become aware that the path to fulfillment begins with the transformation of the caterpillar into a butterfly.

"The path to fulfillment begins with the transformation of the caterpillar into a butterfly."

And it was certainly not at school that I could have taken this course. My parents had enrolled me in Dutch-speaking schools, which was very good from an intellectual point of view. After all, I lived in the capital of a trilingual country, and a Dutch-speaking school education guaranteed me a promising future. But from an emotional point of view, the inflexibility, demands and competition in these schools could only reinforce the self-criticism of the little girl who was already failing to live up to her potential when she wanted to be perfect.

If parents and school do not teach us to love ourselves, we still have a small chance to learn from society. But what are the messages we constantly receive from this society running after time? "We get nothing for nothing", "Life is hard", "We can't make mistakes", "It's too good to be true"... We hear these sentences from our uncles and aunts, we read them in the newspapers, we hear them on television. They are presented to us daily in an insidious and unconscious way, to such an extent that they influence our choices without us noticing. These messages become beliefs and these beliefs limit us. Stress, anxiety, pressure, discipline, rigor and difficulty are part of everyday life and we believe that this is completely normal, because we get nothing for nothing. Societal beliefs do not emphasize slowness, calm, listening, benevolence towards others and especially to oneself. How can you dare to love yourself and show compassion to yourself when you constantly hear that life is hard and that "you have to struggle to get there"?

Now that I had decided to learn to love myself, I could only rely on myself to find out how to do it. Fortunately, life has done a good job by putting people in my path who have opened the way for me. Thank you, Padma. Thank you, Tara. Thank you, Mike. Thank you, Dolores. Thank you, Richard. Thanks to these masters, I have replaced difficulty with ease, criticism with acceptance, doubts with trust and fear with Love.

So, where do we start? Let's start by taking care of ourselves. This attitude can be perceived as selfish. Yet, it is the royal road to a more harmonious world. Rumi's famous quote suggests that "Yesterday I was smart, so I wanted to change the world; today I am wise, so I change myself". Changes come from within, because the outside world is only a reflection of everything that is happening within us. Taking care of yourself is ultimately a sign of generosity. What I mean by "taking care of yourself" is showing kindness to yourself at all times, in all circumstances. It's about becoming your best friend. It's about treating yourself like you would treat someone else. It's about spoiling yourself like you would spoil others. It's listening to yourself like you would listen to your best friend. It's about offering compassion. It's about loving yourself deeply. Developing self-love is a lifelong task, because this love fluctuates over the years and sometimes within the same day. We can start by saying to ourselves "I love and accept myself" because loving ourselves is totally accepting ourselves. We can repeat it more than once a day: "I love myself deeply and I accept myself fully". A little voice may tell you that it is stupid, too simple to be true and "blah blah blah", because we have learned to roll our eyes in the face of too much Love, but try it anyway. You will see for yourself that something is happening inside you. To say that we love ourselves, to do what we love, to surround ourselves with the people we love is essential on the path of self-acceptance and self-love.

First of all, let's marry ourselves

Self-Love is key to a fulfilling life. If our relationship with ourselves is easy, our relationships with others will be even easier. It also helps us to face the dynamics of life, to follow its ups and downs without suffering them but by swinging with them. In fact, we should consider marrying ourselves so that we can promise to always be there for ourselves. It seems rather funny when presented like this, but it is the greatest gift we can give ourselves, and it will positively influence all our relationships. Yes, choose yourself, marry yourself first. It is this love for yourself that will attract the love of others, and more particularly the love of someone special. When you choose yourself for life, write vows to yourself: these can be summed up in the famous formula "In joy as in sorrow. In wealth and poverty. For better or for worse". What could these vows say if you decided to marry yourself?

In joy as in sorrow

This first vow suggests to welcome our duality. Our pleasant emotions as well as our unpleasant emotions. Our qualities and defects. Our strengths and weaknesses. We promise to love ourselves unconditionally as we are. It doesn't matter if it's happy or difficult days. We will stay there, by our own side. We will support ourselves and do what is necessary to let the light shine through the shadows. We will be there for ourselves; we will hold our hands to get through the trials and tribulations and we will be caring towards our duality.

In wealth and poverty

Let's forgive ourselves. We make mistakes and we will make some more. These are *only* learnings. Let us be proud of our progress, of the way we get back on our feet every time. Let us forgive ourselves for going down the wrong path from time to time, because it is this wrong path that allows us to discover treasures, to experience new things and to learn. Let us thank ourselves for making mistakes from time to time. These are the richest experiences.

For better or for worse

Let's take care of ourselves. Let us avoid illness, sadness, unnecessary suffering by taking care of ourselves every day. Preventive medicine is on the rise today, because we finally understand that prevention is the way to avoid healing. Let's take care of ourselves while having fun. Let's have fun practicing a sport. Let's have fun in the kitchen discovering improbable recipes or burning our cake. Let's have fun by expressing our gratitude for the previous day. The joy in these activities makes them even more beneficial. Let's be there for ourselves and add fun to it.

When we are married to ourselves, we don't ask ourselves if others love us. We no longer seek to please, because we already have the Love of the most important person in our lives: ourselves. We then question how others make us feel, what they bring us, and we choose to surround ourselves with the right people for ourselves. Our perspective changes, our choices change, and this attitude of respect and self-love only attracts the respect and Love of others.

This reminds me of the day I met the first person to whom I chose to open my heart again, the man I already told you about. I understood why I had attracted my ex-husband into my life. I had grown up from this experience and deeply accepted that I had lived it for my own good. I forgave myself too. I loved myself and finally accepted myself. I wasn't in a hurry to meet someone because I was comfortable with myself. A man in my life would be the icing on the cake, but not the whole cake. I had become my own cake.

The morning of our encounter, I treated had booked an energy massage. The masseuse quickly told me that the person on her table was no longer the same as before. She also felt that I had evolved over the past few months by giving myself all the attention I needed. She felt that I was finally in the right place. As I left, she smiled at me and said, "You know, the right person is there for you somewhere. He's getting ready for you. He'll come to you when you're ready". I hadn't asked her anything, but I smiled and thanked her. That same evening, a charming young man approached me at a birthday party. We quickly found ourselves having an exciting discussion that lasted all evening. I wasn't wondering if he liked me. I didn't care if he liked me. I simply appreciated the fact that I felt good in his company. I was living in the present moment and enjoying it fully, without hoping for more. The love for myself had attracted to me the love of another. And you know the rest of the story. Today, we have even moved in together.

Unconditional love in the couple

When this unconditional love for yourself attracts the love of another person who positively changes your whole life, you must also succeed in instilling this unconditional love in the couple. It means accepting the other exactly as they are, without expectations. But to be honest, we always have expectations... Whether they are conscious or not. It is good to take a look at them and ask yourself: what do I expect from him/her? For what reason am I with him/her? Is it for my well-being or because I love him/her deeply? What do I want with him/her? How do I project myself? When you dare to look at yourself honestly, you are sometimes surprised to find unspoken expectations that create unnecessary disappointments. Once your expectations are cleared, you can accept the other person entirely and love him or her for everything he or she is, with all his or her qualities and faults. We can smile at their clumsiness, distraction or anger, even if it sometimes makes us go out of our minds. We are only humans, after all.

Whenever this is the case, you can see it and choose again to love the one chosen by your heart unconditionally. Their shortcomings also have a purpose: they are part of their path and will make them grow. To love them unconditionally is to be there to help them when they are faced with their weaknesses. It is to avoid judging them on the way they react, think, choose. It is to let them be free to become who they are supposed to become.

Loving our duality

We are not perfect, and it is perfect like that. We are made of dualities. Small and tall. Good-looking and ugly. Generous and selfish. Bright and dark. We are human, and this humanity needs duality. We need our qualities as much as our faults, our strengths as our weaknesses. We need our weaknesses and flaws because they transcend us. It is by learning to accept them and accept ourselves as we are, to love ourselves deeply with our shadow and light, that we discover unconditional love. The unconditional love for oneself from which follows the unconditional love for others. We accept and love the other in all his or her entirety, exactly as he or she is. In this whole and living love, we give ourselves. We also develop our gifts to benefit others and put ourselves at their service.

Let's not wait to change to love ourselves. Let's not wait to become this perfect being in order to finally love ourselves. Let's accept the magnificent being that we already are. Let's accept that we are a duality and that there is room for improvement. It is a joy that there is always room for improvement, and this path is perfect as such.

« Don't be afraid of perfection. You'll never reach it. »
Salvador Dali.

When we completely accept ourselves, we love ourselves and fill ourselves with joy. This joy allows us to grow through various positive events that we attract to ourselves. Joy attracts joy. Let's be happy to be who we are, let's not seek to be someone else, because all the others are already taken. Our wounds are rooted in us, but fun, joy, pleasure, wonder are the beautiful side of the coin. They help us recharge our batteries, fill us with hope and love to face life's upheavals. They make these events less painful, lighter and help us to take a step back. Joy brings us more love for ourselves and allows us to heal our wounds. Growing it on a daily basis is the best gift you could give yourself. Whenever you find yourself falling back into a slant or criticizing yourself, love yourself more, have fun with these bad habits, smile at them. Try to improve a little, but still accept the perfectly imperfect being that you are. The peace of the soul comes from the total acceptance of oneself.

Healing through Love

The body is an incredibly intelligent machine that knows how to take care of itself. It knows how to heal, and the energy of Love is enough to stimulate the healing process that we all have within ourselves. This love leads to the healing of all wounds, whether physical, emotional, mental or spiritual. Once we are on this path of healing and acceptance, we can move mountains and have the life we dream of. We attract the best people, the best situations, the best jobs, the best homes, the best life partners who will vibrate with the same frequency of love, acceptance and kindness as the one we emit.

Today we can regain our full power and realize that the events of the past and the emotions of today still linked to these events of the past, however painful they may be, are part of the past. Even if they have deeply hurt us, we can choose not to let them lead our lives anymore, because we are in the present moment and not in the past. We can now welcome them, honour them and then transmute them and thus show love for ourselves.

"When we enter the unity of Love, healing begins and everything that must happen, happens."

Little by little, as Love grows, we enter a state of unity. We feel fulfilled and complete. We no longer seek to satisfy our needs from the outside, but we look inward where we know that all our resources are located. We are whole and we feel in full connection with others. Our emotions are more pleasant than unpleasant. Transmutations are becoming rarer and rarer, and our vibratory rate is rising more and more, attracting to us everything we need. Love will have released the weight from our shoulders, healed our wounds. We will have regained our power and discovered that we have absolutely everything in us. We have joy, happiness, trust, love, success, abundance, compassion, forgiveness, reconciliation, the ability to evolve to be who we really are. We have everything in us. You have what it takes to become the person you dream of.

Of course, we may not agree with these ideas. Our free will allows us to decide how to live. Our School offers us a field of experience that we choose to live or not. We choose absolutely everything, starting from our inner world. We may choose to renounce certain events and their lessons. We can choose to grow up with the obstacles that life poses on our path. We have full power to decide what we do with life's difficulties and how we approach them: they are opportunities to deeply become ourselves and to love ourselves. They are steppingstones, detours in the right direction, gifts of Life.

How do we do this in practice?

Steps 3, 4 and 5 of the Self-Healing Spiral have the final goal of increasing self-love. When we take care of ourselves, when we approach ourselves with kindness and give ourselves all the attention we need, we are in Love. Do all the exercises in these steps that bring you peace and joy. Find out what works best for you. Since we are all different, the suggested exercises can be adapted to your needs and feelings. Listen to yourself and do what feels right for you. This will restore your power. If you want more, here are some suggestions to love yourself even more:

. . .

Suggestions to love yourself even more

- Do the Meditation of Infinite Love every morning (see Chap. 6)
- Repeat the following sentence several times a day: "I love myself, I accept myself, I forgive myself, I am Enough"
- Compliment yourself every day in front of the mirror
- Make a list of your successes, qualities or gifts
- Eat foods that make you happy
- Do the sport you prefer or treat yourself
- Learn to say no when a feeling of heaviness invades you
- Be true, authentic and sincere. Don't pretend
- Treat yourself as you treat your best friend
- Smile. Feel how this lip movement changes your inner state
- Accept your flaws, they are part of you and they are beautiful too
- Comfort yourself, show compassion for yourself
- Accept your emotions, let them flow through you

What we learned in this chapter:

- The body knows how to heal itself physically, emotionally, mentally and spiritually. Love is enough to initiate this healing process.

- To love yourself is to accept yourself exactly as you are now, with your faults and qualities
- Love is learned and developed little by little by taking care of yourself and treating yourself like you'd treat your best friend: with respect, trust, support, kindness...
- Marry yourself before you really get married
- Cultivate joy in your life: it is a form of Love

8

PRACTICAL CASES

The Self-Healing Circle is the first part of our method called the Self-Healing Spiral. An event triggers us and we find ourselves at the step of the Circle: The Wound. Then, the other steps follow and we now know how to live and go through each of them. All the tools and knowledge that you have been given will help you to consider your emotions as a conversation, to discover and love yourself more. I hope they will bring you as much as they have brought me.

As you have just seen, this Circle consists of six steps. Three steps are practical. These are active steps compared to the other three steps that are inactive. Indeed, The Wound, Emotion and Love are steps you are experiencing and going through. The other three steps, Welcome and Honour, Transmute and Practice will impact the three inactive steps. This dance, this permanent exchange leads us to the form of a Spiral, because we will go through the Wound several times, but every time at a different degree. Wounds have several layers we are going to peel like onions.

Furthermore, three steps reveal rather uncomfortable emotions (Wound, Emotion, Welcome and Honour) and three others give way to comfortable emotions (Transmutation, Practice and Love). This balance reflects the balance of Life in which we are constantly moving. Some days, some weeks we are in the dark part of the picture and others we are filled with joy and wonder. Let us take advantage of these moments of grace to recharge our batteries and take a step back from to the difficulties we are facing.

Now let's see what the Self-Healing Circle looks like with some concrete cases so that you can, you as well, implement it in your life.

First case : The overcooked cookies

One autumn afternoon, I'm baking cookies. Having always loved cooking, I tend to follow my

intuition rather than the recipe and the clock in my stomach rather than the one hanging on the wall. I'm enjoying this activity that relaxes me and I'm already looking forward to this little attention that will fill the gourmet stomach of my boyfriend and mine too, of course. I put the cookies in the oven and go to the living room to read a book.

Twenty minutes later, I take a first look at the oven. The cookies are still very white. They are not golden enough as I like them to be. I go back to my exciting reading. Several minutes pass before I go back to admiring my cookies. Now they're golden brown. I quickly take them out of the oven, burn myself on the way (yes, I am clumsy) and place them on a round plate. My creation of the day in hand, I am heading to the dining room, which acts as an office and places the plate of cookies next to my boyfriend's computer. Impatient, I help myself while they are still softened by the heat. He waits to finish his email before helping himself. The cookies cool down quickly and become as hard as concrete. I overcooked them and kind of knew it when taking them out of the oven. It was also visible at their brownish colour. A cookie is expected to be tender and soft. He takes one and jokingly says : "How long did you go back to reading on the couch?"

I take it personally because I know they're overcooked. They're too hard to be pleasant to eat and it frustrates me, because I wanted to please us. The intention is there, but the result is completely unsuccessful. I'm going to the couch and grumble. He's a few meters from me and laughs at seeing me so frustrated for something so futile. The more he teases me, the more I feel like a loser. I get the urge to cry and flashbacks come up. I'm boiling within and get angry. I'm completely overreacting, but the images coming to mind are showing me why. These visions from the past make me realize that my emotion is not related to the current situation, but to a past event. Our emotions are often memories of the past (see Chapter 3.).

These images bring me back to an autumn evening of the previous year. I had spent more than an hour in the kitchen preparing a delicious vegetable and salmon lasagna. My ex-husband tended to criticize the dishes I cooked for him when they were not to his liking. Our tastes being different, it was often "disgusting and inedible" to his eyes. I didn't appreciate it when he would then get up to make Aïki Noodles when I had just spend hours preparing the meal. Yet at the time, I didn't say much and kept my frustration to myself.

Realizing this, I regained my power by using the Self-Healing Spiral instead of remaining hurt by this past event. I was able to accept the flood of tears that filled my eyes and should have come out more than a year ago.

Let's take a step-by-step look at this.

1. WOUND :
Rejection. It is not necessary to know your wound to use the Self-Healing Spiral. It is
obviously better to be aware of it, but since this step is inactive, you are simply going through it. It will be expressed through step two, the Emotion. If you want to discover your wound, then click on this link who will lead you to me website : www.eleonoredeposson.com/what-mask-is-preventing-you

2. EMOTION :
I felt rejected by the teasing comments about overbaked cookies. I perceived them as
critics and felt like a loser, not good enough for him. I wanted to hide away (mask of the
fleeing, see chapter 2) and cry. My emotion was exacer-

bated by the fact that I had not been able to express the same emotion during a previous but similar situation. Although this situation was much lighter, I reacted as if they were the same. I released an emotion from the past through the cookies of the present.

3. WELCOME & Honour:

I welcomed the sadness and let the tears roll down. I honoured the emotion by thanking it for showing me that this wound was still there. I let the loser-feeling overwhelm me for several minutes by telling myself in silence:

"Yes, I'm sad and I feel like a loser. I was overly criticized by someone who didn't respect me. It is normal that I feel that way, because his attitude wasn't loving. But I am there for myself and welcome the sadness.Thank you emotion for coming to see me today. Thank you for opening the door to myself. Thank you freeing me from the weight of the past."

4. TRANSMUTATION :

The fourth step transforms the sadness into a pleasant emotion, fills our lack of love and rewires our beliefs. I prepared for the transmutation by repeating twice:

"I now choose to enter a space of peace and tranquility by transforming the nature of my emotion."

For 2 minutes, I repeated the following sentence out loud, then for 3 minutes, in a low voice, while visualizing it with love and acceptance for myself. I then repeated this step for 21 days in a role :

"Today, I, Eléonore, love myself deeply and accept myself exactly as I am. »

5. PRACTICE :

I still felt a little tension in my body and practiced 20 minutes of gentle yoga in the living room. As a yoga teacher, I improvised the practice, but you can find the perfect practice to release emotions on my youtube channel. Search "Eléonore de Posson + Yoga".

6. LOVE :

The attention I gave myself through the active steps 3, 4 and 5 has increased the Love I feel for myself. This healed the wound to bring it closer to full recovery. I felt soothed and relieved. The next time my cookies are overbaked and someone points it out to me, I won't take it personally anymore and accept that I am perfectly imperfect and that it is perfect like that.

Second case : The lost love

One of my friends, whom we will call Sophie here, often uses the Self-Healing Spiral to deal with all her emotions. She told me that this method had finally allowed her to

welcome her emotions and understand why it's so important to do so. It has been a year since Sophie and her partner
separated. They meet for coffee and she realizes she is still
in love with him. A few days later, she starts panicking,
thinking she'll never get over him. She's afraid he won't try
to win her back. She even fears never being able to be happy
without him and feels like her life has stopped since he left.
This fear is so strong that she finds herself being paralyzed,
not knowing what to do.

She then decides to apply the Self-Healing Spiral:

1. WOUND :

Sophie doesn't know what her main wound is. Neverthe-
less, she decides to heal herself with this new method she
just learned.

2. EMOTION :

Fear. Sophie panics because she hasn't been able to deal
with her emotions before. She feels lonely, lost, helpless
regarding this desire for them to get back together. She's
afraid she won't be happy without him and miss out on her
life.

3. WELCOME & Honour:

Sophie decides to welcome the emotion. She sits on her
bed and takes a deep breath before letting the emotion
come up. She cries and lets fear, sadness, loneliness inhabit
her. She feels the emotion circulate. She takes the time to

experience it, then puts her hand on her heart and says to herself:

"Yes, I am afraid. I'm afraid I can't live without him. I'm afraid I'll never be happy. I'm afraid I'm not going to get away with it and miss out on my life. I'm sad and I feel so lonely. I'm so scared. But I am there for myself and welcome the fear. Thank you emotion for coming to see me today. Thank you for opening the door to myself. Thank you for freeing me from this burden of the past."

4. TRANSMUTATION :

She then shifts the fear of being alone and unhappy to giving herself love and trust with the transmutation :

"Today, I, Sophie, know that I will meet the right person at the right time and I love myself deeply."

She repeats this sentence 2 minutes aloud, then 3 minutes, in a low voice, while visualizing herself hand in hand with a man, without focusing on his former companion. Then she repeated this sentence for 21 days, all day long, while walking in the woods, cooking, running,...

5. PRACTICE :

She finished the Self-Healing Circle with the meditation of infinite love, while holding the sign of Infinite Love on her heart. You can also find the meditation here: www.eleonoredeposson.com/freetools

6. LOVE :

Sophie is feeling better. Fear has weakened even though she feels that it is still present and that she will still have to remove the other layers of her emotions. She feels more at ease. She now masters her emotions instead of letting them control her.

Combination of tools

In the example of the cookies mentioned above, these are the tools that have been used:

Step 3: WELCOME: "Talking to Yourself"
Step 4: TRANSMUTE: "Transmutation"
Step 5: PRACTICE: "20 minutes of gentle yoga"

Many associations are possible. Below are some other examples, but I suggest you choose the tools with which you feel most comfortable and finally make your own combination. You have the choice for steps 3 and 5, knowing that step 4 only has the Transmutation tool.

The ideal is to carry out step 3 and 4 one after the other, then if possible to continue with step 5, but the latter can also be done later in the day.

Step 3: WELCOME: "Write"
Step 4: TRANSMIT: "Transmutation"

Step 5: PRACTICAL: "Meditation of Infinite Love & Gratitude"

Step 3: WELCOME: "Speak to the concerned person"
    Step 4: TRANSMIT: "Transmutation"
    Step 5: PRACTICAL: "Anuloma-Viloma"

Step 3: WELCOME: "Write"
    Step 4: TRANSMIT: "Transmutation"
    Step 5: PRACTICAL: "Energy healing treatment"

How long does it take?

In the example of the cookies, it took less than 40 minutes to apply all 3 tools. If you listen to yourself and get used to using the tools, the circle can be completed in 20 to 40 minutes.

However, this same tour may last longer. It depends on how much time you will give yourself to go through the active steps and apply the different tools. A frustrating event at the office can be released only in the evening when you are alone at home and can devote yourself to the different tools.

You can complete steps 3 and 4 as soon as the event occurs and step 5 only later in the day or even the week. It all up to you and the time at your disposal.

. . .

Step 5 can also be performed without any particular link to an event. Indeed, its double objective allows you to apply its tools when you feel like it. You don't need to be facing a difficulty to take care of yourself.

Panic attack or strong emotions?

In the case of strong emotions, if you feel the panic attack coming or the mind running in a loop, you can start by calming yourself down with the Anuloma-Viloma breathing exercise (see Chapter 6). In a few moments, you'll be back on your feet. This tool allows us to find an emotional balance quickly and prepares us for the work of the Self-Healing Circle.

Once you have calmed down, you are ready to start the Self-Healing Circle and its active steps 3, 4 and 5. Make sure you are in a caring environment and be compassionate to yourself when applying the Self-Healing Circle after a panic attack. You'll be sensitive, it's a good time to take care of yourself as gently as possible. If you don't have the energy, give yourself a few hours to allow you to welcome what caused the strong emotions and replace them with softness and love. The tools are there, waiting for the right time for you.

First : Calm the Panic attack

Perform Anuloma-Viloma breathing for 5 to 10 minutes. This will bring your body and your mind back to a peaceful state. It will relax your body, which will then tell your mind that everything is fine. Then, later in your day, choose the right time to apply the Self-Healing Circle with as much compassion and care as possible. You'll still be feeling fragile from this panic attach so apply the tools gently, with as much care as possible. You can be really proud of yourself for doing the first steps to heal.

Then : Apply the Self-Healing Spiral
    Step 3: WELCOME: "Talking to Yourself"
    Step 4: TRANSMIT: "Transmutation"
    Step 5: PRACTICAL: "Meditation"

Just in a bad mood?

You've been in a bad mood for a few days. You don't really know why. You can also use the Self-Healing Circle without any particular purpose. Your moody mood blocks you at step 2 of the circle, so simply continue by applying steps 3, 4 and 5 to free yourself from it. You can always use the next sample sentences to make you feel better in a few minutes.

Step 3. Start by talking to yourself. You can repeat the following sentence several times. You can complete it with what sounds right to you. Give yourself about ten minutes in this step:

"Yes, I'm not fine. Something's not right. Something's bothering me. I feel sad/tired/moody/... and it's normal. I give myself the right to feel sad/tired/moody. It happens. It just goes through me. Thank you bad mood for opening the door to myself."

Step 4. Continue by repeating this sentence for 3 minutes:
   "Today, I, (your first name), choose to let go. I love and accept myself exactly as I am."

Step 5. Finish with the exercise of your choice: 20-minute yoga, Meditation of infinite love or Breathing Anuloma-Viloma, (see chapter 5). If you have your own exercise to relax, feel free to use your own tool. It can be singing, drawing, going for a run, ... anything allowing your body to relax is good at this point.

Application advice

- Apply the Self-Healing Spiral as soon as an event upsets you or provokes unpleasant emotions such as stress, anxiety, fear, anger, sadness, disgust...
- You can also do the Self-Healing Spiral if you feel moody for no apparent reason.
- Choose a tool for each active step (Welcome, Transmutation, Practice), that resonates most with you.
- The 3 active steps of the Self-Healing Circle can be performed in 20 to 40 minutes if you apply them one after the other.

- The more you practice the circle, the more naturally it will come to you.
- The alternate breathing, Anuloma-Viloma, from step 5, can be performed immediately if you are experiencing intense emotions. This will calm you down and you will then be able to perform steps 3, 4, 5 in order.

9

THE SELF-HEALING SPIRAL

The Self-Healing Spiral is the result of several Self-Healing Circles navigated. The circles follow one another as we go through the same wounds several times to heal them. If we suppress our emotions or don't know what to do with them, we will at best stagnate in the middle of the Spiral, at worst, descend to the bottom of the Spiral by accumulating unpleasant emotions.

The more we go around the Self-Healing Circle and follow all its steps, the more we climb up the Self-Healing Spiral. This self-care increases our vibratory rate, the is the speed at which our energy circulates. The faster it circulates, the higher its frequency. This attracts to us situations and people having the same frequency. All this, making us more fulfilled, happy and joyful.

"If you do not face your shadow, it will come to you in the form of your destiny."
Carl Jung[1]

This quote from Carl Jung explains that everything that does not come to our consciousness comes to us through the events of life. Over the years and its hardships, life will open our eyes to who we are, what we fear and all the shadows we wish to avoid. Why? Because we attract these events to us. Why? Because fear, doubt and limiting beliefs exist within us and vibrate in our subconscious mind. Why? Because we were hurt in our early childhood or even before that. Why? Because the very purpose of Life is to discover our wounds and to heal them, to welcome our gifts and develop them, in order to become the most fulfilled version of ourselves and love ourselves as we are. Remember our little cloud story? We came to the School of Life to get the diploma of Self-Love. Of course, you may not adhere to this vision, but that doesn't change the fact that we all have parts of shadows and light, faults and qualities, wounds and gifts. We will still have to face challenges that will bring out fears, doubts and uncomfortable emotions. Unfortunately, suffering will always be part of life. Knowing it makes it possible to address these moments with more compassion for oneself and to see these pains as opportunities to discover more about ourself and grow. It also allows us to enjoy more of the good surprises that life has to offer. However, this cannot be learned in no time at all. I still surprise myself pushing away the fear, not wanting to feel the uncomforted and saying "No, I don't want to go there and feel that. It's going to be okay." And then quickly, I realize that it doesn't help me. Quite the opposite.... I then take the time to welcome what is happening within and let the emotion flow through me. I then continue the Self-Healing Circle with steps 4 and 5 and feel better.

We are made from the same mold, but different, so I don't pretend to offer a magic formula. The magic formula is within you. This is a suggestion of how to take care of yourself and create your own formula to face life's difficulties. The purpose of the Self-Healing Spiral is to help you face these difficult times and heal yourself little by little. It will help you manage your emotions, discover yourself and love yourself. And I include myself entirely in this description, because we're never done with loving ourselves.

· · ·

The Self-Healing Spiral works like the Law of Attraction. The higher you rise up the Spiral by soothing your wounds with compassion and love, the more you attract what you need to heal. Furthermore, the more you master your thoughts to turn them into a creative power, the more synchronicities will help you on your path. Either way, by playing with the Law of Attraction or by taking care of yourself, you climb into the Spiral and experience more joy and success. It may seem confusing in its simplicity, but I have experienced it many times.

The Law of Attraction

The Law of Attraction is a universal law. This law explains that we attract events through our vibrations. We experience the vibrations already existing within us, because no energy is lost, but everything transforms. Every second we vibrate like a lake on which we have just thrown a rock. The movements of the water will vary depending on the stone, its size, weight, etc. Life events will impact our vibrations, depending on the way we experience them, their weights, their consequences, our perception of them,... These vibrations in turn will attract other events to us and so on. Our thoughts transforming into actions are all pure energy. When we think of something, we emit an energy, a vibration, a frequency. All of these are synonyms. The energy that you emit is not lost, it simply transforms and attracts to you other energies, which we call actions, events, situations or people.

. . .

If you are familiar with this law, this seems obvious to you. But for those who discover the Law of Attraction, I would like to illustrate this explanation with an example. Observe a pan of water. The water is there, you can see it, drink it, touch it with your fingers, right? If you subject the water pan to a strong heat, it will turn into steam and disappear. Yet the water was there a few minutes earlier. Has it really disappeared? No, it has turned into steam that is no longer visible, drinkable or touchable. Yet, it is. It also works the other way around by placing the water pan in the freezer. Then the water will turn into ice. Water changes appearance according to its environment and what it is submitted to. The same is true for our energy, which changes in appearance according to its environment: from thinking into emotion, emotion into action, action into situation.

The Intention goes beyond the Action

Action is strongly promoted in our Western society. However, the Law of Attraction suggests that an element is even more powerful than action. The intention. Carlos Castaneda, American anthropologist and author, tells us that "In the Universe, there is an indescribable and immeasurable force called the intention. Everything that exists is connected to the intention. This mainly means that there is no point in acting if the intention behind it isn't the right one. If you ask your boss for a promotion, because you want to buy an apartment, but you don't really like your work, because you've always dreamed of being a great cook. It is likely that this promotion will never come to an end. The intention behind it is signed by lack, envy, despair, perhaps revenge or other negative feelings. On the other hand, if you carry out the same request with an intention of joy, abundance and gratitude, because this job teaches you a lot of things and your colleagues are great, you have more chances to get what you want. When our actions are tinged with positive intentions, their result will come from the same range of positive colours. So, pay attention to the intentions motivating your actions. What is really hiding behind your actions?

American writer Wayne Dyer reveals the 7 facets of intention[2]. According to him, it would be enough to act with one of these intentions to create a harmonious and prosperous life. Nurture yourself with one of these to ensure a positive result to your action:

- **Creativity.** Be creative when life doesn't go in the direction you want and have confidence that these are just detours in the right direction.
- **Goodness.** Be good to yourself and to others. Goodness flows from one person to another and comes back to you like a boomerang.
- **Love.** We were created by Love and we are fundamentally, pure love. Demonstrate your ability to love with kindness, cooperation rather than competition and envy.
- **Beauty.** See how beautiful Life is. The flowers in the park next door, the imperfections of the face of a friend, the colours of your meal... Beauty is everywhere once you start to see it.
- **Expansion.** The Universe is constantly expanding. Grow with it as you develop

emotionally, intellectually and spiritually. This reading already offers you expansion.

- **Abundance.** Be abundant. Be generous to yourself and to others. Abundance will simply come back to you. Also, behave as if you have already achieved the expected result. Feeling the abundance is key to attract it in your life, because your life matches your inner vibration, right? Be abundant and don't set the intention from a place of lack and despair. This will also help you to let go of the final result and just feel the abundance right here, right now, that's already in your life.
- **Receptivity.** Dare to receive. Learn to reach out when you receive a gift from a person or from life. Seize what comes to you. Be grateful every day for receiving more.

Imagination goes beyond reason

If we cannot act yet, we can already imagine. Another important element of the law of Attraction is the visualization. Visualization allows us to create mental images of the object of our desire. We will see ourselves, as precisely as possible, experiencing our dream: the promotion, the new car, the new apartment, Prince Charming... As we have already seen in Chapter 5 on Transmutation, the brain does not make a distinction between an event we have actually experienced and thoughts of that experience. Just thinking of an accident can scare us. Our thoughts vibrate and sometimes re-traumatise us.

But we can also use them to our advantage. The things you see and the images you create are processed the same way by your brain. The more you bring your attention to something you want, the more you imagine it, the more likely it is to occur according to the law of Attraction. Here are two visualization exercises that you can apply today to start changing your life :

5 desires Visualization

Step 1: Determine 5 things you want to see in the medium term. (6 to 18 months)

Step 2: Find 5 images that represent these 5 things. You can print them from the internet or have a look in magazines.

Step 3: Collect these images and make them into a wallpaper for your phone, your desktop or a collage that you will put in a place where you go every day (fridge, bathroom mirror,...)

Here is my wallpaper and my 5 projects:
- Stay centered and grounded
- Teach my knowledge for the well-being of everyone
- Share my experiences while using my passion for writing
- Growing old alongside a man with whom I share a true love
- Living in a modern, eco-responsible home where, one day, I will be able to offer the comfort to beautiful children.

Do you know how many times a day we check our phones? An American study has shown that we unlock our phone an average of 80 times a day. This means 6 times an hour if we consider using our phone for 13 hours. Every ten minutes, then. This is huge! If every time you look at your phone you consciously think about these 5 things you dream of having, they will definitely happen sooner or later.

Conscious Visualization

Step 1: Sit comfortably in a quiet place you like. You can raise the frequency of the room by burning incense, a candle or playing relaxing music.

Step 2: Feel one of the 7 characteristics of intention: Creativity, Kindness, Love, Beauty, Expansion, Abundance, Receptivity.

Step 3: In this state of mind, think about what you want to see in the coming months. The more you will be precise, the greater the strength of the intention will be. If you wish to attract Love to yourself, think of the sensations it gives you. Walks hand in hand, exciting conversations... but don't imagine a particular person. Trust that the right person, the right job, the right house will come to you. Do this exercise for 10 to 15 minutes, 21 days in a row.

Gratitude is a magnet for happiness

To express your Gratitude is to bring our gaze to the outside and observe all the little things providing us satisfaction. By thanking everyday events and elements, we train our memory to remember the luck we have, rather than the risk we take. We focus on positive things rather than negative things. It is enough to see for yourself what Gratitude creates in you. Try this:

Think of a delicious meal you've shared lately. It might be with a friend you hadn't seen in a long time and shared a meal with. Express your gratitude for the choice of food we have in our Western countries and the friendship you keep on building with this beautiful person. You had a good time so it is easy to express your Gratitude in this case. Feel the dancing of your cells, the lightness, the joy that grows as you say "Thank you".

Now think of a meeting at the office that lasted for hours. You came out of there with a headache and a pile of things to do before the end of the day. What do you feel in yourself? Tight stomach? Body tension? This feeling will be heavier. Yet Gratitude can lighten it. Try it, preferably, to think about the challenge this work brings you, what you learn, where it can lead you in the future. Think about when someone will notice your excellent work. It may be your boss, a colleague or a customer. The Gratitude emitted on this day will make your feeling of heaviness much lighter and will focus your attention on what this job brings you rather than the energy it takes away from you.

To whom do we express our Gratitude? If it is something tangible, you can express your gratitude to the person who gave something to you. The neighbour who held the front door, the baker and her fresh bread, the bus driver, the colleague who taught you something, the attentive ear of a friend, the tenderness of your partner,... If it is less tangible things, you can express your Gratitude to the Universe, Mother Nature, The Source, God, your Guides,... Choose the name you feel the most comfortable with, it doesn't really matter. In fact, you can thank this "entity" for everything that put a smile on your face. As much the baker and her fresh bread as the sun on your skin in the middle of winter. As surprising as it may be, He/She has ears and will hear you.

The American psychologist and author of the book *THANK YOU! When gratitude changes our lives,* Robert Emmons teaches us that two conditions must be met to express your gratitude correctly:

   - First, the recognition of the moment or thing for which we are grateful

   - Then, the observation that it comes from outside oneself

.   .   .

Once these conditions are met, we can say "THANK YOU" to everything bringing us a small or large amount of satisfaction. The more thanks we spread around us, the more our entourage will feel valued by our recognition and will return this form of love to us. Obviously, the intention behind these thanks must be sincere. Remember the power of intention explained just a few lines ago. Human beings also have sensors for lies, so just be authentic.

From a physical point of view, your brain will become stronger with recognition and will notice more and more the things you can be grateful for. This attitude will gradually lead you to astonishment, because you'll start to realize how lucky and abundant you already are.

From a quantum point of view, Gratitude is an emotion with high frequencies. The vibrations of gratitude will come back to you like a boomerang, because nothing is lost and everything is transformed... Be ready to live other moments that will make you jump for joy, because again, "He" has ears.

Gratitude Exercise

Before going to bed, list 10 things you are grateful for. It can be the sun on your skin, a nice conversation with a friend, a healthy body, a good laughter at work, a received compliment or the pretty sweater you just got yourself. List everything that made you smile or brought you some satisfaction.

You can also go to my website to download a free meditation for gratitude. It's 5 minutes long and will be ideal to create a feeling of abundance and gratitude before going to bed. Download it at eleonoredeposson.com/freetools

This Gratitude exercise will show you that life is made of many beautiful things and that we shouldn't take everything for granted. This attitude will raise your frequency and you know what that means by now.

In addition, it has been proven that listing positive things before going to sleep helps calm the mind. Bringing our attention on pleasant things rather than the bills to pay provides a deeper and more regenerating sleep. We do two birds with one stone!

In a few pages, you have just become familiar with this Law of Attraction. The proposed exercises will help you get more what you want and you now understand the importance of your thoughts and intentions.

The Self-Healing Spiral works together with the Law of Attraction. The more we have taken care of our wounds and have given Love to ourselves, the higher our vibratory rate will be. We will then attract other happy events. Of course, we are never protected from uncomfortable events, because these are supposed us make us to grow and open our eyes on our unhealed wounds. It is uncomfortable to grow but sop much worth it.

Moreover, by juggling with the Law of Attraction, you rise up the Self-Healing Spiral and life gifts you with events or people helping you heal. Indeed, you can rise up the Spiral by taking care for yourself and your emotions, but you can also ascend the Spiral with the exercises of the Law of Attraction, which will help heal yourself. Your healing comes from two poles: your personal investment and the happy events of Life. All the work doesn't just come from you. You take care of yourself, but Life does too. Because Life wants what's best for you. It sometimes has a curious ways of showing it, but I've seen it a lot of times. My divorce was the best thing that happened to me! Even though, it took me some time to acknowledge it.

How do you realize that you are descending the Self-Healing Spiral?

We are often caught up in the movement of life with solicitations, demands, stress, pressure we're the ones putting on ourselves. We're not always aware that day after day, something is missing and making us feel more and more exhausted. Until one day, where we wonder what we did to get there?

How do we realize that we are descending the Self-Healing Spiral? Mainly by observing ourselves and bringing awareness to how we feel. We could spot some of the following signs:
- Doubts, lack of confidence
- Anxiety, fear of the future
- Nervousness
- Emotions that take over
- Stress
- Melancholy
- Sullen mood
- Lack of/small appetite
- Insomnia

.   .   .

We constantly ascend and descend the Self-Healing Spiral because of life's events, but alcohol, lack of sleep and an unbalanced nutrition will also make these signs appear much faster.

To go back up, we have several choices:

- Go through the steps of the Self-Healing Circle
- Apply a tool from step 5 (Yoga, Meditation, Pranayama, Care)
- Carry out an exercise of the Law of Attraction (Visualization, Gratitude)

Choose the option or exercise that speaks most to you, but you can also set up a little routine in your daily life. Here are the different times of the day when you can integrate the exercises of your choice:

Early Morning
Transmutation
Infinite Love Guided Meditation
Silent Meditation and Visualisation

Throughout the day, when stressed
Anuloma-Viloma

Throughout the day, when facing uncomfortable emotions
Apply the Self-Healing Spiral :

Step 3 : Write and burn the paper
Step 4 : Transmutation
Step 5 : Gentle Yoga, as soon as possible

In the evening
Yoga
Gratitude Exercise

If having insomnia
Anuloma-Viloma

Once a week
Walk in nature
Visualisation
Journal, writing your intentions down
Enjoy a nice meal with close friends

Once a month
Energy Healing

Day after day, all these exercises from the Self-Healing Spiral will help you to feel more fulfilled, to face difficulties, to have more confidence in yourself and the future, to heal your wounds and to love yourself. That's what they helped me with. Let's go back to the first little exercise of this book.

. . .

After going through these chapters, ask yourself again, on a scale from 1 to 10:
    -How much do you trust yourself?
    -How much do you accept yourself?
    -How much do you love yourself?

Have these figures changed? Are they evolving? How would you like to change them? What tools would help you in the growth of these results?

Inner Peace

We all seek serenity. If you're having this book in your hands, it's probably because you are looking for a little bit of a breather, some sweetness or serenity. We do retreats, meditate, read inspiring books, go on holidays hoping to find some peace. This quest has been ours since the night of time. My own journey has made me realize two things: the first is that this peace can only come from inside. We quickly cling to external solutions, but they are only ephemeral. While a real work on ourselves, done with patience and compassion, makes it possible to reach this peaceful state. Peace envelops us when healing comes. When our wounds are healed, we are at peace. The one and only path to inner peace is the path of healing. It seems obvious now, but I had to start this healing journey myself to understand it.

    Healing brings us the much coveted serenity, because we then dare to see our dark sides, converse with them, learn from them, take care of ourselves and move towards self-acceptance. Little by little, we love ourselves, for better or worse. But this path is rocky. Challenges await us. They push us to choose ourselves over and over again. Then, other days seem to be moments of grace. We are getting closer to inner peace. Life offers us a foretaste of it, because we are beginning to make peace with ourselves. We forgive ourselves, we accept ourselves, we love ourselves and we are developing our gifts that bring us so much joy.

Then life happens again, reviving some old wounds. This gives us the opportunity to discover ourselves even better. At this point, we know the path of healing, the path of self-love and can more easily go through it again. We initiate this journey with more confidence, because we know how to navigate it and what awaits us at the end.

The Self-Healing Spiral helps us walk through the rocky path of life. It helps us manage our emotions and teaches us that we have all the power to be happy and at peace. The Self-Healing Spiral is now in your hands. Its tools and knowledge are yours. You can implement them anytime, anywhere throughout your life.

I wish you to enjoy all these tools to colour your life with joy, abundance, love and peace. Always remember that you already have everything in you.

What we learned in this last chapter:

- The Self-Healing Spiral works like the Law of Attraction
- Intention, visualization and Gratitude are key to using the Law of Attraction to your advantage

- The Law of Attraction attracts positive events helping your wounds to heal
- The more you work on your wounds, the more you ascend into the Self-Healing Spiral. The higher you are, the more beautiful things happen to you.
- The healing path is the only path leading to inner peace
- Don't forget to download all the free tools available for you on my website. Enjoy! eleonoredeposson.com/freetools

THANK YOU

My heart is filled with emotion, that I welcome of course, when thinking of all the people that made this book possible. I am so grateful and feel really lucky to have received so much support. This book wouldn't exist without any of them and I feel quite small when writing this :

Thank you Rich, my love. Thank you for your support since the beginning of this adventure, when this book was only an idea. Thanks for your guidance, your time, your ideas and the English corrections. Thank you for allowing me to share a little bit about our story. Thank you for being you.

Thank you Michele, Caroline and Marianne, three psychologists and coaches, for supporting this method and giving me more information about the human brain. Sharing the first draft of the Self-Healing Spiral with you was priceless to me!

Thank you Petra, for the beautiful drawings you did. You captured exactly how I imagined our little "Coco", our inner child. You made a fantastic job at transforming my ideas into touching drawings.

Thank you to all my friends and family who took a lot of time reading, correcting, commenting the French version of this book, making all this dream possible.

Thank you, dear reader. Without you, I couldn't share my passion, my experience and realize my purpose. Thank you for going through these pages. I hope they brought some light into your days!

PERSONAL NOTES

....
....
....
....
....
....
....
....
....
....
....
....
....
....
....
....
....
....
....
....

Personal notes

....

....

....

....

....

....

....

....

....

....

....

....

....

....

....

....

....

....

....

....

....

....

....

....

....

....

....

....

....

....

....

....

Personal notes

....
....
....
....
....
....
....
....
....
....
....
....
....
....
....
....
....
....
....
....
....
....
....
....
....
....
....

Visit my website to find more info and free tools:
www.eleonoredeposson.com/freetools

Don't hesitate to drop me an email and let me know how
you liked the book : ele@eleonoredeposson.com

More everyday tips on Instagram and FB @eledeposson

You are also invited to join my private FB group for weekly
videos, tips, exercise and a beautiful community of like-
minded women :

Women Awakening to Self animated by Elé de Posson

NOTES

The Self-Healing Circle

1. EMOTO, Masaru. Love Thyself: The Message of Water. New York, Hay House, 2006, 176 pages.
2. LASKOW, Leonard. Healing with Love: A Breakthrough Mind / Body Medical Program for Healing Yourself and Others. Authors Choice Pr, 2 edition, 2007, 341 pages.

2. Step 1: The Wound

1. Dolorès Lamarre is the founder of the Dolores Lamarre Insitute+, near Montreal in Quebec. She teaches different energy practices such as Reiki and SAIME. She is also the author of various books, some of which are bestsellers: *Le temps de lâcher prise* (The Time to Let Go), and *Êtes-vous Victime-Bourreau-Sauveur?* (Are You Victim – Executioner – Saviour?)
2. Bourbeau, L. (2013). The 5 wounds that prevent you from being yourself. Saint-Jérôme, Québec: Edition Pocket.
3. Deepak Chopra is an Indian author, a pillar in alternative medicine. He has written numerous bestsellers and created the Chopra Center where they teach meditation, yoga, etc.
4. Dr Leonard Laskow is a doctor who studied at the University of Stanford. He has studied for over 30 years the healing power of love. He created the term "holoenergetic" that refers to healing with the energy of "the everything".

    subresidance, Healing with Love. (2012, January 3) *Healing with Love* [Video file]. Retrieved from https://www.youtube.com/watch?v=Slj4ZIfCWBY

3. Step 2: The Emotion

1. Frazer, B. (2014) *E-motion*. USA: Gaia. Retrieved from: https://www.gaia.com/video/e-motion
2. McLaren, K. (2010). *The Language of Emotions: What Your Feelings Are Trying To Tell You.* Boulder, CO: Sounds True.

3. Joe Dispenza is a reputed American chiropractor, lecturer and author. He is also a member of the Quantum faculty at the University of Honolulu, The Omega Institute for Holistic Studies in Rhinebeck, New York as well as the Kripalu Center for Yoga and Health in Massachusetts.
4. McLaren, K. (2010). *The Language of Emotions: What Your Feelings Are Trying To Tell You.* Boulder, CO: Sounds True.
5. Bodanov, S, (2016). *Loi de l'attraction: mode d'emploi: vers le bonheur, le succès et la réussite. [Law of attraction: a manual guide: towards happiness, success and achievement].* Chêne-Bourg (Swiss): Jouvence éditions.
6. Martel, J. (2015) *Le grand dictionnaire des malaises et des maladies.* [The Big Dictionary of Difficulties and Illnesses]. Aubagne: Quintessence.

4. Step 3: Welcome & Honour

1. Gabrielle, B. (2018). *The Universe Has Your Back: Transform Fear to Faith.* Carlsbad, CA: Hay House, Inc.

Complementary tool: Grounding

1. I thank Dolores Lamarre for this image that accompanies me daily.

5. Step 4 : Transmute

1. DISPENZA, Joe. Breaking the Habit of Being Yourself : How to lose your Mind and Create a new one. New York, Hay House, 2012, 329 pages.
2. PASCUAL-LEONE A., Modulation of muscle responses evoked by transcranial magnetic stimulation during the acquisition of new fine motor skills, Human Cortical Physiology Unit, National Institute of Neurological Disorders and Stroke, Maryland, USA, 1995.
3. Don Tolman est un auteur américain, spécialiste des sagesses anciennes. Cette phrase est un extrait du document *E-motion*, réalisé par Frazey Bailey en 2013.

6. Step 5 : Practice

1. LOEHR, Jim et SCHWARTZ, Tony. The Power of Full Engagement. New York, Shubhi Publications, 2003, 254 pages.

2. SALAMON, Maureen. The Science of Yoga and Why it works. (Article en ligne). England, Live Science, 2010, https://www.livescience.-com/35129-yoga-increases-brain-function-bone-density.html

3. GABA is the abbreviation for gamma-aminobutyric acid. It is the main neurotransmitter of the central nervous system of mammals and therefore the human being. It has inhibitory effects, i.e. it prevents anxiety-related neural hyperactivity.

4. STILES, Tara. Why is No-Pain-No-Gin so common ? (Online article). New York, Strala Yoga, 2018, http://stralayoga.com/be/bad-life-strat-egy-no-pain-no-gain-common/

5. TAYLOR, Michael. Michael Taylor on moving well & living in align-ment. (podcast). New York, Mindbodygreen, 2018, https://player.fm/se-ries/the-mindbodygreen-podcast-2428356/ep-83-michael-taylor-co-founder-of-strala-on-moving-well-living-in-alignment

Tool 3.2: Meditation

1. RICARD, Matthieu. L'art de la méditation. Paris, NiL éditions, 2008, 150 pages.

2. BOORSTEIN, Sylvia. Don't Just Do Something, Sit There: A Mindful-ness Retreat with Sylvia Boorstein. San Francisco, HarperOne, 1996, 146 pages.

3. NEWBERG, Andrew et D'AQUILI, Eugène. Why God won't go away : Brain Science and the Biology of Belief. Ballantine Books, New York, 2002. 240 pages.

4. NEWBERG, Andrew. How do meditation and prayer change our brains. (Article en ligne). Philadelphia, Andrew Newberg, 2014, www.andrewnewberg.com/research.

5. ANONYME. 3 expériences religieuses au microscope. *Science et Avenir*. Paris, September 2003.

6. GABRIEL, Roger. Meditation : The What, Why and How. (Online arti-cle). Carlsbad, The Chopra Center, 2018, https://chopra.com/arti-cles/meditation-the-what-why-and-how.

7. NICHITECU, Radu. 3 Practical Tips for begginers meditators. (Online article). Carlsbad, The Chopra Center, 2017, https://chopra.com/arti-cles/3-practical-tips-for-beginner-meditators

8. FRAZER, Baily. E-motion. (documentary). USA, Gaia, 2014, 85 minutes. https://www.gaia.com/video/e-motion

Tool 3.4: Energy Healing

1. S.A.I.M.E stands for Système d'Aide et d'Intervention à la Médecine Energétique (System of Assistance and Intervention in Energy Medicine). This institute was founded by Dolores Lamarre, author and lecturer from Quebec.
2. HUYGHEN, Sandra. De la Science à la Conscience, chemin initiatique d'éveil et de guérison. Liège, Tedx, 2017, 20 minutes. https://www.youtube.com/watch?v=uLpBGCX5LFs

9. The Self-Healing Spiral

1. Carl Jung is a Swiss doctor, psychiatrist, psychologist and essayist. He is the founder of Analytical Psychology who suggests the analysis of the unconscious and the human soul, i.e. the individual psyche.
2. DYER Wayne. The power of intention: Learning to co-create your world your way. New York, Hay House, 2011, 312 pages.

Made in the USA
Lexington, KY
11 November 2019

56848356R00131